International Economic Growth

Contributions to Economics

Peter R. Haiss
**Cultural Influences on
Strategic Planning**
1990. ISBN 3-7908-0481-9

Manfred Kremer/Marion Weber (Eds.)
**Transforming Economic Systems:
The Case of Poland**
1992. ISBN 3-7908-0585-8

Marcel F. van Marion
Liberal Trade and Japan
1993. ISBN 3-7908-0699-4

Hans Schneeweiß/
Klaus F. Zimmermann (Eds.)
Studies in Applied Econometrics
1993. ISBN 3-7908-0716-8

Gerhard Gehrig/
Wladyslaw Welfe (Eds.)
Economies in Transition
1993. ISBN 3-7908-0721-4

Christoph M. Schneider
**Research and Development
Management:
From the Soviet Union to Russia**
1994. ISBN 3-7908-0757-5

Bernhard Böhm/
Lionello F. Punzo (Eds.)
Economic Performance
1994. ISBN 3-7908-0811-3

Michael Reiter
The Dynamics of Business Cycles
1995. ISBN 3-7908-0823-7

Michael Carlberg
**Sustainability and Optimality
of Public Debt**
1995. ISBN 3-7908-0834-2

Lars Olof Persson/Ulf Wiberg
Microregional Fragmentation
1995. ISBN 3-7908-0855-5

Andreas Foerster
**Institutional Analysis
of Development Administration**
1995. ISBN 3-7908-0853-9

Ernesto Felli/Furio C. Rosati/
Giovanni Tria (Eds.)
**The Service Sector: Productivity
and Growth**
1995. ISBN 3-7908-0875-X

Giuseppe Munda
**Multicriteria Evaluation in
Fuzzy Environment**
1995. ISBN 3-7908-0892-X

Boris Maurer
**R & D, Innovation and Industrial
Structure**
1996. ISBN 3-7908-0900-4

Giovanni Galizzi/Luciano Venturini
(Eds.)
**Economics of Innovation:
The Case of Food Industry**
1996. ISBN 3-7908-0911-X

David T. Johnson
**Poverty, Inequality and Social
Welfare in Australia**
1996. ISBN 3-7908-0942-X

Rongxing Guo
Border-Regional Economics
1996. ISBN 3-7908-0943-8

Oliver Fratzscher
**The Political Economy of Trade
Integration**
1996. ISBN 3-7908-0945-4

Ulrich Landwehr
**Industrial Mobility and Public
Policy**
1996. ISBN 3-7908-0949-7

Arnold Picot/Ekkehard Schlicht
(Eds.)
Firms, Markets, and Contracts
1996. ISBN 3-7908-0947-0

Karin Peschel (Ed.)
**Regional Growth and Regional
Policy Within the Framework
of European Integration**
1997. ISBN 3-7908-0957-8

Thorsten Wichmann
**Agricultural Technical Progress and
the Development of a Dual Economy**
1997. ISBN 3-7908-0960-8

Ulrich Woitek
Business Cycles
1997. ISBN 3-7908-0997-7

Michael Carlberg

International Economic Growth

**With 136 Figures
and 23 Tables**

Physica-Verlag
A Springer-Verlag Company

Series Editors
Werner A. Müller
Peter Schuster

338.91
C278i

Author
Prof. Dr. Michael Carlberg
Department of Economics
Federal University
Holstenhofweg 85
D-22043 Hamburg, Germany

A printing grant by Federal University, Hamburg, is gratefully acknowledged.

ISBN 3-7908-0995-0 Physica-Verlag Heidelberg

Cataloging-in-Publication Data applied for
   Die Deutsche Bibliothek – CIP-Einheitsaufnahme

Carlberg, Michael: International economic growth: with 23 tables / Michael Carlberg.
Heidelberg: Physica-Verl., 1997
   (Contributions to economics)
   ISBN 3-7908-0995-0 brosch.

The use of general descriptive names, registered names, trademarks, etc. in this publication does not imply, even in the absence of a specific statement, that such names are exempt from the relevant protective laws and regulations and therefore free for general use.

Softcover Design: Erich Kirchner, Heidelberg

SPIN 10565840   88/2202-5 4 3 2 1 0 – Printed on acid-free paper

Preface

We live in a world where capital is free to move. Increasingly this determines the pattern of international growth. Savings are invested in the country yielding the highest return, thus adding to its stock of capital. This development is especially true of common markets such as the European Union, which are based on free trade and financial openness. The present monograph deals with international growth, featuring the dynamics of foreign debt and domestic capital.

I had many helpful talks with my colleagues at Hamburg: Michael Schmid (now at Bamberg), Franco Reither, Wolf Schäfer, Thomas Straubhaar and Johannes Hackmann. In addition, Michael Bräuninger and Philipp Lichtenauer carefully discussed with me all parts of the manuscript. Last but not least, Doris Ehrich did the secretarial work as excellently as ever. I wish to thank all of them.

Contents

Economists have, in some sense, always known that growth is important. Yet at the core of the discipline, the study of economic growth languished after the late 1960s. Then, after a lapse of nearly two decades, this research became vigorous again in the mid-1980s.

Robert J. Barro, Xavier Sala-i-Martin

Growth theory traditionally has treated each country as if it were an island unto itself. Extensions of the theory to a world with international trade and capital flows have been left as esoteric exercises for algebra lovers. If ever this practice was defensible, surely it is no longer.

Gene M. Grossman, Elhanan Helpman

Although most of the legal barriers to international capital mobility are now gone, the world capital market remains essentially segmented along national lines. Capital may be free to move internationally, but its owners and managers prefer to keep almost all of each nation's savings at home.

Martin Feldstein

Introduction

Very recently, there has been a renaissance of growth theory. Of course, the engine of economic growth is capital formation. In this connection, two stylized facts can be observed: 1) the globalization of capital markets and, at the same time, 2) the segmentation of capital markets.

Against this background, the present monograph deals with international borrowing and lending. The framework of analysis is given by the theory of economic growth. Particularly, it proves useful to consider the Solow model, the overlapping generations model and the infinite horizon model. The focus will be on the dynamics of foreign debt and foreign assets. By making use of phase diagrams, we shall look into the steady state and its stability. Moreover, we shall keep track of the processes of adjustment induced by diverse macroeconomic shocks. Take for instance an increase in the saving rate, a rise in the rate of labour growth, or a one-time technical progress. They raise a lot of questions: How do foreign debt and domestic capital move over time? What does the chain of cause and effect look like?

In conducting the analysis, it is helpful to review different scenarios: the small open economy and two large countries. Capital mobility is either perfect or imperfect. As a rule, labour is supposed to be immobile. As an exception, however, labour mobility is allowed for. In general, wages are flexible, but they can also be fixed. Both exogenous and endogenous growth are treated.

This is clearly reflected in the exposition. Chapter I is concerned with the small open economy, chapter II is on two large countries. In chapter III capital mobility is restricted, in chapter IV labour mobility is introduced, in chapter V wages are fixed, and in chapter VI growth becomes endogenous. For the remainder of the introduction, the exposition will be laid out in greater detail. This will be followed, in the next section, by a brief survey of the literature.

Let us begin, in chapter I, with a small open economy under perfect capital mobility. For the small open economy, the foreign interest rate is given exogenously. Under perfect capital mobility, the domestic interest rate agrees with the foreign interest rate. Some emphasis will be placed on a Solow model, featuring the dynamics of foreign assets. The income of domestic residents is composed of factor income and the interest inflow. Households save a certain proportion of their income. Net exports and the interest inflow make up the surplus on the current account. The current account surplus in turn contributes to the accumulation of foreing assets. This gives rise to a number of questions. Does a steady state exist and, if so, will it be stable? Will the small open economy be a creditor or a debtor? Does it run a surplus or deficit on its current account (trade account, for that matter)? What will be the effect of an increase in the saving rate on capital per head, output per head, foreign assets per head and consumption per head? Similarly, how does a shock in the rate of labour growth or in the foreign interest rate impinge on the small open economy?

In chapter II, we turn to two large countries with perfect capital mobility. Under perfect capital mobility, the interest rate of country 1 coincides with that of country 2. At first, in section 1, we shed some light on the case of different saving rates. The investigation is based on an overlapping generations model with identical technologies and equal rates of labour growth. Which of the countries will be a creditor, and which a debtor? Which of the countries will run a surplus on its current account, and which a deficit? And what about the trade account? Further contemplate an increase in the saving rate of country 1. How are capital per head, output per head, foreign assets per head and consumption per head affected by this, in each of the countries, respectively?

Then, in section 3, we discuss technical progress abroad. The reform countries in Central Eastern Europe and the new industrial countries in South East Asia are going to enter the world market. What will be the consequences for the advanced countries? What does this imply in terms of capital flows and consumption? We start from a two-country model, country 1 including the advanced countries and country 2 the emerging countries. The disturbance just mentioned can be interpreted, within the setting of the model, as a one-time technical progress abroad. Specifically, we rely on a Solow model with equal saving rates and equal rates of labour growth. Now what will be the influence of a rise in the efficiency of country 2 on capital per head, output per head, foreign assets per head, and consumption per head, in each of the countries, respectively? Finally, in section 4, we study different rates of labour growth. We postulate an overlapping generations model with equal saving rates and identical technologies.

Does a steady state exist and, if so, will it be stable? Which of the countries will be a creditor, and which a debtor?

So far, we assumed perfect capital mobility. Instead, in chapter III, we assume imperfect capital mobility. Obviously there is a high risk in lending abroad, as contrasted with lending at home. This risk consists mainly in the political risk and the currency risk. Therefore lenders have an incentive to impose a contraint on lending abroad. This can be modelled in either of two ways. 1) The foreign debt of a country must not exceed a critical level, expressed in terms of its capital stock as a collateral (maximum feasible debt-capital ratio). 2) The interest rate paid by the borrowing country to the lending country is an increasing function of the debt-capital ratio. In section 1, we regard a Solow model of a small open economy characterized by a fixed debt ratio. The basic idea is that an increase in domestic capital allows the country in question to incur more foreign debt, thereby allowing a further increase in domestic capital. Take again a rise in the saving rate. How are capital per head, output per head, foreign debt per head, and the interest rate affected by this?

In chapter IV we introduce labour mobility. International growth increasingly involves labour migration. Labour moves to the country which offers the best wages. This development is especially true of single markets such as the European Union, which are based on free trade and unhampered factor movements. Here a Solow model comprising two countries with perfect capital mobility serves as a point of reference. We have equal saving rates, equal rates of labour growth and identical technologies. Under perfect labour mobility, wage rates agree across countries. Thus marginal products of labour are the same across countries, too. When there is no labour mobility, the given allocation of labour determines the allocation of capital and output. On the other hand, when there is indeed labour mobility, the allocation of labour, capital and output becomes indeterminate. This, however, is inconsistent with empirical evidence. Therefore we postulate a third, immobile factor, say land. Then the given allocation of land governs the allocation of labour, capital and output. Now the reasoning goes as follows. At first prohibit labour mobility. Let the marginal product of labour in country 1 exceed that of country 2, so the wage rate of country 1 is greater than that of country 2. Then permit labour mobility. Accordingly, labour moves from country 2 to country 1. This lowers the wage rate in country 1 and raises the wage rate in country 2 until the wage rates balance. What does this mean in terms of capital flows and consumption? Who will win and who lose?

In chapter V, we peg the wage rate. Initially let the economy be in a steady state with full employment. In this condition, the wage rate is driven up. This reduces labour demand, so unemployment occurs. That is why output, income, savings, investment and capital formation come down. What will be the impact on the growth rates of capital, labour demand and output? And what about foreign assets as well as consumption? The analysis is carried out within the framework of a small open economy. One after another, we suppose perfect capital mobility, imperfect capital mobility and land as an immobile factor.

To conclude, in chapter VI, we address endogenous growth. The investigation is performed within the socalled AK model. Firms produce a homogeneous commodity by making use of both physical and human capital. Raw labour (i.e. labour without human capital) is unproductive. Correspondingly it does not enter the production function. First catch a glimpse of the small open economy with perfect capital mobility. Let productivity surpass the foreign interest rate, hence there will be an extremely large capital inflow. On these grounds, the stock of capital tends to explode. Of course, this is grossly unrealistic. Next have a look at the small open economy with imperfect capital mobility. Again let productivity exceed the foreign interest rate, so the country will be a debtor. In these circumstances, imperfect capital mobility can be defined by a fixed debt ratio. What will be the effect of an increase in the saving rate (in productivity, in the foreign interest rate or in the maximum debt ratio, respectively) on the growth rate of capital? Will the small open economy grow faster than the closed economy?

Alternatively, let productivity fall short of the foreign interest rate, thus the country will be a creditor. How can imperfect capital mobility be viewed here? Once more there is a high risk in lending abroad, so lenders impose a constraint on it. The foreign assets of a country must not exceed a critical level, expressed in terms of its capital stock (maximum feasible foreign asset ratio). Again regard a hike in the saving rate (in productivity, the foreign interest rate or the maximum foreign asset ratio). What will be the consequences for the growth rate of capital? Will the small open economy evolve more rapidly than the closed economy?

Last but not least, consider two countries with imperfect capital mobility. Let the productivity of country 1 be greater than that of country 2, and let the saving rates be the same across countries. In this situation, country 1 will be a debtor and country 2 a creditor. The foreign assets of country 2 must not surpass a critical level, expressed in terms of its capital stock. In the steady state without capital mobility, the growth rates are constant, the growth rate of country 1 being higher than that of country 2. Then introduce capital mobility. Will this equalize growth rates?

Brief Survey of the Literature

There is a well-established body of literature on international economic growth. Let us begin with the Solow model, which is marked by a proportional saving function. Generally, perfect capital mobility is assumed here. Domar (1950) is an early forerunner in dynamic theory. He deals with the effect of foreign investment on the balance of payments. The framework is given by a simple dynamic model of a small open economy. He argues that a capital outflow generates an interest inflow. Now if the foreign interest rate exceeds the growth rate, then, in the steady state, the interest inflow will be larger than the capital outflow. Accordingly, the country in question will be a net importer of commodities. Borts (1964) considers a small open economy with an ad hoc investment function. There are both traded and nontraded goods, so the terms of trade enter the scene. He concentrates on the process of adjustment set in motion by an increase in the world demand and world price of the traded good. He demonstrates that, as a response, output grows faster than labour input. Amano (1965), too, regards a small open economy. The focus is on the transitional dynamics of introducing capital mobility. As a result, national income develops more rapidly than labour. The paper treats only dynamics, and not the steady state. Negishi (1965), in a very short mathematical paper, has two countries with different saving rates but equal rates of labour growth. He shows that, in order to reach the optimum, the government should levy a tax or grant a subsidy. Hamada (1966), in a rather extensive paper, studies two countries with identical technologies. He distinguishes several cases, e.g. different saving rates or different rates of labour growth. He proves the existence of two steady states, one of them being stable, the other unstable.

Hanson and Neher (1967), by means of a diagram, find out the golden rule of a small open economy. When the foreign interest rate lies above the growth rate, the optimal saving rate will be very large. The other way round, when the foreign interest rate lies below the growth rate, the optimal saving rate will be zero. Neher (1970, 1971) takes a small open economy with a general production function. Emphasis is laid on the foreign position and the balance of payments. He discusses both the steady state and dynamics. Fischer and Frenkel (1972) start from a small open economy with a cost-of-adjustment investment function. There are consumer goods as well as capital goods. The accent is put on the trade in debt and capital goods. Gale (1974) has two countries with different technologies but equal rates of labour growth. He centres on net exports (imports). Hanson (1974) is based on a small open economy. The supply of external funds depends on the debt-capital ratio. On this premise, he derives the optimum of international lending and borrowing. Onitsuka (1974) also rests on a small open economy. The saving rate is a function of the world rate of interest, the expected rate of profit, as well as the capital stock. The limelight is on the stages in the balance of payments, especially with respect to the mature creditor country. Hori and Stein (1977) have two countries, where country 1 completely specializes in consumer goods and country 2 in capital goods. They examine free trade in equities and goods. The paper by Koizumi and Kopecky (1977) rests on a small open economy. They posit that a rise in the foreign ownership of domestic capital leads to a rise in the transfer of technical knowledge. Ruffin (1979) considers two countries that differ in technology. The transfer problem and the stages in the balance of payments are at the centre of interest. The monograph by Carlberg (1995) is concerned about the sustainability and optimality of public debt. He reviews the closed economy, the small open economy and two countries, building on the Solow model, the overlapping generations model and the infinite horizon model.

At this point we leave the Solow model and turn to the overlapping generations model (Diamond 1965). The overlapping generations model in a sense is characterized by intertemporal optimization within a finite time horizon. Buiter (1981) takes two countries with unequal time preferences. He shows that the country with the higher time perference runs a current account deficit. Besides he probes into the transition from financial autarky to openness and its welfare effects. Persson (1985) investigates the consequences of budget deficits for intergenerational welfare. The setting is given by the small open economy as well as two countries. Schmid and Großmann (1986, 1990) regard two countries that disagree in time preference and technology. By working out phase diagrams they look into dynamics. There are a savings shock and a productivity shock. Finn (1990) simulates a stochastic model of a small open economy. The monograph by Frenkel and Razin (1992) is devoted to fiscal policy in the world economy. The book by Ihori (1996) addresses public finance, among other things for two countries. The key subjects are tax reform, the negative spillovers of a consumption tax, capital income tax, optimal taxation and spending.

The next point refers to the class of Ramsey (1928) models. Hamada (1966) inquires into a small open economy with an infinite horizon. There foreign debt per head is not allowed to go beyond a certain fraction of capital per head. Bardhan (1967), too, has a small open economy with an infinite horizon. He supposes that an increase in foreign debt per head causes an increase in the interest rate. Likewise, Hamada (1969) has a small open economy with an infinite horizon. Again the interest rate moves up as foreign debt per head moves up. Wan (1971) develops a very complex model, the time horizon being either finite or infinite. Bade (1972) has a small open economy with a finite horizon. The accent is on optimum foreign borrowing with restricted mobility of capital. Bazdarich (1978) studies a small open economy with an infinite horizon and a borrowing constraint. There are two sectors, one producing a consumer good, the other a capital good. The focus is on the stages in the balance of payments. Giavazzi and Wyplosz (1985) have a small open economy with an infinite horizon. They impose no borrowing constraint. Instead, they assume that the discount rate corresponds to the difference between the foreign interest rate and the labour growth rate. Siebert and Van Long (1987, 1989) take a small open economy with a finite horizon. Their major themes are: 1) the half and the full debt cycle, 2) sensitivity analysis with respect to the planning horizon. The monograph by Blanchard and Fischer (1989) contains a section on the small open economy with an infinite horizon and cost to installing capital. They establish both the command optimum and the decentralized optimum. Emphasis is placed on the steady state, dynamics, and a productivity shock. Eaton (1989) presents a survey on the small open economy with an infinite horizon. He stresses the role of the intertemporal budget constraint, the solvency constraint and the transversality condition. Devereux and Shi (1991) have two countries with infinite horizons. Another special feature is that the rate of time preference is endogenous. Barro, Mankiw and Sala-i-Martin (1995) contemplate a small open economy with an infinite horizon. The Cobb-Douglas production function has three inputs: physical capital, human capital, and raw labour. The authors distinguish between two cases, perfect or imperfect capital mobility. In the second case, foreign debt per head must not surpass some limit. This seems to be consistent with empirical findings. The advanced textbook by Barro and Sala-i-Martin (1995) has a chapter on the small open economy. The table of contents includes: rationing of international credit, variations in time preference, finite horizon, adjustment cost for investment. Obstfeld and Rogoff (1995), in a handbook article, draw on a small open economy. Relying on a two-good model, they discuss quite a number of aspects: comparative advantage, output fluctuations and investment, nontradables, consumer durables, the terms of trade and the transfer problem, demographic structure and fiscal policy.

We come now to endogenous growth. It was started or resumed by Romer (1986). He examines a closed economy with increasing returns and knowledge as an input. Alogoskoufis and van der Ploeg (1991) have two countries inhabited by overlapping generations that are infinitely lived. The authors demonstrate that capital mobility contributes to the equalization of growth rates. Moreover they shed some light on budgetary policy. Buiter and Kletzer (1991) take two countries with common technology and free capital mobility. Persistent differences in growth rates are due to private thrift, public debt, capital taxation and the policy towards human capital. The monograph by Grossman and Helpman (1991) deals with innovation and growth in the global economy. Rebelo (1991) argues that cross-country differences in government policy bring about cross-country disparities in growth rates. Rivera-Batiz and Romer (1991) model the trade in goods and the flow of ideas. Solow (1991) delivers a report on the state of the art. Rebelo (1992) places emphasis on developing countries. He asks why growth rates do differ. In answering this question, he dwells on government policy, trends in the rate of growth, international trade and poverty traps. In addition he talks about international capital markets. Pack (1994) writes on the intellectual appeal and the empirical shortcomings of endogenous growth theory. Van der Ploeg and Tang (1994) treat budget deficits as well as research and development in the global economy. The keynotes are convergence or divergence, knowledge spillovers, investment and trade-promoting policies. Romer (1994) presents an overview on the origins of endogenous growth. Solow (1994) offers a rather critical appraisal of endogenous growth theory. The textbook by Barro and Sala-i-Martin (1995) is mainly on the closed economy. The authors build one-sector and two-sector models, paying special attention to the role of human capital. Further topics are: expanding variety of products, improvements in the quality of products, diffusion of technology, labour supply and population. Schneider and Ziesemer (1995), confining themselves to the closed economy, ask what's new and what's old in new growth theory.

The next point relates to the empirics of economic growth and imperfect capital mobility. Let us begin with economic growth. Dowrick and Nguyen (1989) inquire into OECD comparative growth from 1950 up to 1985. Particularly they take account of catching-up and convergence. Barro (1991) evaluates a cross section of 98 countries, spanning the period 1960-1980. In the first line he wants to explain the growth rate of per capita GDP. Regression analysis yields that human capital has a positive influence, whereas the initial level of per capita GDP and the share of government consumption in GDP have a negative influence. Barro and Sala-i-Martin (1992) rely on data for the US states from 1840 until the present. They indeed observe convergence, but diminishing returns to capital set in very slowly (as compared to the neoclassical model of the closed economy). Mankiw, Romer and Weil (1992) examine human capital, while Fagerberg (1994) investigates technology.

We now proceed to empirical research on imperfect capital mobility. The paper by Feldstein and Horioka (1980) refers to the OECD countries 1960 - 1974. The authors establish that the saving rate differs from the investment rate by 1% on average, which is surprisingly low. From this they conclude that international capital flows are very small. They attribute this finding to portfolio preferences and institutional rigidities. This paper has stimulated a lot of research and discussion (e.g. Feldstein 1983, 1991, 1994, 1995, Murphy 1984, Obstfeld 1986, 1995, Ghosh 1995, Lewis 1995).

Last but not least, there is an extensive literature on default risk, capital flight and debt relief (e. g. Cooper and Sachs 1985, Cohen und Sachs 1986, Lucas 1990, Cohen 1991, 1994, Mohr 1991, Kletzer 1994, Eaton and Fernandez 1995). This line of thought will not be taken up here.

CHAPTER I. SMALL OPEN ECONOMY

1. Solow Model

1.1. Foreign Assets

1.1.1. Steady State

The analysis will be conducted within the following framework. Firms produce a single commodity Y by means of capital K and labour N. For ease of exposition, let technology be of the Cobb-Douglas type with constant returns to scale $Y = K^{\alpha} N^{\beta}$, $\alpha > 0$, $\beta > 0$ and $\alpha + \beta = 1$. Full employment does always prevail. Domestic output can be devoted to consumption, investment and net exports $Y = C + I + X$. Labour grows at the natural rate $\dot{N} = nN$ with $n = $ const. Here the dot denotes the time derivative $\dot{N} = dN / dt$ with time t.

For the small open economy, the foreign interest rate is given exogenously $r^* = $ const. Under perfect capital mobility, the domestic interest rate agrees with the foreign interest rate $r = r^*$. Firms maximize profits $\Pi = Y - rK - wN$ under perfect competition, where Π stands for profits and w for the wage rate. As a consequence, the marginal product of capital is determined by the interest rate $\alpha Y / K = r$. This, in turn, yields the desired stock of capital. Conversely, the wage rate is governed by the marginal product of labour $w = \beta Y/N$.

We come now to capital dynamics. $Y = K^{\alpha} N^{\beta}$, $\alpha Y / K = r$ and $\dot{N} = nN$ can be stated in terms of growth rates: $\hat{Y} = \alpha \hat{K} + \beta \hat{N}$, $\hat{K} = \hat{Y}$ and $\hat{N} = n$. Here the hat symbolizes the growth rate. From this follows immediately $\hat{K} = \hat{Y} = n$. Put another way, capital and output grow at the natural rate. It is worth emphasizing that this holds in the momentary equilibrium, and not only in the steady state. Investment adds to the stock of capital $\dot{K} = I$, so the result can be expressed as $I = nK$.

The next point refers to the dynamics of foreign assets. Domestic residents earn the interest rate r on foreign assets F, hence the interest inflow amounts to rF. The income of domestic residents consists of factor income and the interest inflow $Y + rF$. Households save a certain proportion of their income $S = s(Y + rF)$ with $s =$ const. The income of domestic residents serves for consumption and savings $Y + rF = C + S$. Accordingly, the consumption function is $C = (1 - s)(Y + rF)$. The current account surplus is defined as the sum of net exports and the interest inflow $E = X + rF$. The current account surplus, on its part, contributes to the accumulation for foreign assets $\dot{F} = E$.

Thus the model can be represented by a system of eight equations:

$$Y = K^{\alpha}N^{\beta} \tag{1}$$

$$r = \alpha Y / K \tag{2}$$

$$Y = C + I + X \tag{3}$$

$$C = (1 - s)(Y + rF) \tag{4}$$

$$I = nK \tag{5}$$

$$E = X + rF \tag{6}$$

$$\dot{F} = E \tag{7}$$

$$\dot{N} = nN \tag{8}$$

Here α, β, n, r, s, F and N are exogenous, while C, E, $\dot{F}$, I, K, $\dot{N}$, X and Y are endogenous.

It is useful to do the analysis in per capita terms. The production function can be written as $y = k^{\alpha}$ with capital per head $k = K/N$ and output per head $y = Y/N$. The interest rate equals the marginal product of capital $r = \alpha y / k$. $y = c + i + x$ takes the place of (3), where $c = C/N$ is consumption per head, $i = I/N$ is investment per head and $x = X/N$ is net exports per head. The consumption function can be stated as $c = (1 - s)(y + rf)$, with foreign assets per head $f = F/N$. $I = nK$ is transformed into $i = nk$. The current account surplus per head is the sum of net exports per head and the interest inflow per head $e = x + rf$ with $e = E/N$. Further take the time derivative of $f = F/N$ to get $\dot{f} = \dot{F}/N - F\dot{N}/N^2$. Together with $\dot{F} = E$, this yields $\dot{f} = e - nf$.

In per capita terms, the model can be characterized by a system of seven equations:

$$y = k^\alpha \tag{9}$$

$$r = \alpha y / k \tag{10}$$

$$y = c + i + x \tag{11}$$

$$c = (1-s)(y + rf) \tag{12}$$

$$i = nk \tag{13}$$

$$e = x + rf \tag{14}$$

$$\dot{f} = e - nf \tag{15}$$

Here α, f, n, r and s are given, whereas c, e, $\dot{f}$, i, k, x and y adjust themselves appropriately.

From (9) and (10) one can deduce:

$$k = (\alpha / r)^{1/\beta} \tag{16}$$

$$y = (\alpha / r)^{\alpha/\beta} \tag{17}$$

Capital per head and output per head are invariant, since the interest rate is invariant. This holds not only in the steady state, but also in the momentary equilibrium! Clearly, this differs from the conclusions drawn in the closed economy.

In the steady state, the motion of foreign assets per head comes to a halt $\dot{f} = 0$. So the steady state can be encapsulated in a system of seven equations:

$$y = k^\alpha \tag{18}$$

$$r = \alpha y / k \tag{19}$$

$$y = c + i + x \tag{20}$$

$$c = (1-s)(y + rf) \tag{21}$$

$$i = nk \tag{22}$$

$$e = x + rf \tag{23}$$

$$nf = e \tag{24}$$

Here α, n, r and s are fixed, while c, e, f, i, k, x and y are flexible.

Of course, (16) and (17) are valid in the steady state, too. Hence an increase in the foreign interest rate leads to a decline in capital per head and output per head. On the other hand, a rise in the saving rate has no influence on capital per head and output per head. The same applies to a rise in the rate of labour growth. This forms a remarkable contrast to the closed economy. There, an increase in the saving rate pushes up capital per head, and an increase in the rate of labour growth pulls down capital per head.

Next we shall look into stability. The model can be compressed to a single differential equation $\dot{f} = g(f)$. Substitute (12) and (13) into (11) and solve for x = y − (1 − s)(y + rf) − nk. Then put this into (14) to get e = s(y + rf) − nk. Moreover insert this into (15) to arrive at:

$$\dot{f} = s(y + rf) - nf - nk \qquad (25)$$

Differentiate (25) for f to find out:

$$\frac{d\dot{f}}{df} = rs - n \qquad (26)$$

This gives rise to two cases. If n > rs, then $d\dot{f} / df < 0$, so the steady state will be stable. Conversely, if n < rs, then $d\dot{f} / df > 0$, so the steady state will be unstable. This differs again from the closed economy, where the steady state always proves to be stable.

Empirically speaking, we have n > rs, thus the steady state will indeed be stable. To illustrate this, consider a numerical example with n = 0.03, r = 0.06 and s = 0.1. This implies rs = 0.006. As a rule, the steady state will be stable. However, when the rate of labour growth is very low, the steady state will be unstable. Similarly, when the foreign interest rate (the saving rate, for that matter) is very high, the steady state will be unstable. Henceforth we shall assume n > rs, thus the steady state will be stable.

We turn now to the main properties of the steady state. From (25) together with $\dot{f} = 0$ one can infer:

$$f = \frac{sy - nk}{n - rs} \qquad (27)$$

Besides eliminate k and y in (27) with the help of (16) and (17):

$$f = \frac{(s - \alpha n / r)(\alpha / r)^{\alpha/\beta}}{n - rs} \qquad (28)$$

If $s \gtrless \alpha n/r$, then $f \gtrless 0$. That is to say, the high-saving country will be a creditor. And the other way round, the low-saving country will be a debtor. In full analogy, if $n \gtrless rs/\alpha$, then $f \lessgtr 0$. Put differently, the fast-growing country will be a debtor. On the other hand, the slow-growing country will be a creditor. Likewise, if $r \gtrless \alpha n/s$, then $f \gtrless 0$. That means, when the foreign interest rate is high, the country will be a creditor. Conversely, when the foreign interest rate is low, the country will be a debtor.

In addition, we regard a rise in the saving rate. Owing to (27), this brings up foreign assets per head. And as s approaches n/r from below, f becomes very large. But if $s = 0$, then $f = -k$. In other words, foreign debt per head is equal in amount to capital per head. Correspondingly, figure 1 shows foreign assets per head as a function of the saving rate.

Now contemplate an increase in the rate of labour growth. Due to (27), this lowers foreign assets per head. As n comes close to rs from above, f tends to explode. And if n becomes extremely large, f draws near to $-k$. In this instance, once more, foreign debt per head coincides with capital per head. Figure 2 visualizes foreign assets per head as a function of the rate of labour growth.

Third regard a lift in the foreign interest rate. By virtue of (28), this drives up foreign assets per head. When r approximates n/s from below, f becomes very large. On account of (16), as r comes close to 0, k grows without limits. That is why f becomes extremely small (i.e. minus infinity). Figure 3 depicts foreign assets per head as a function of the foreign interest rate.

20

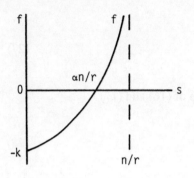

Figure 1
Saving Rate and
Foreign Assets Per Head

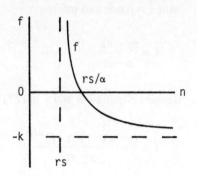

Figure 2
Growth Rate and
Foreign Assets Per Head

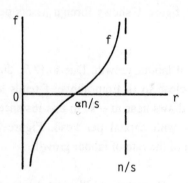

Figure 3
Foreign Interest Rate and
Foreign Assets Per Head

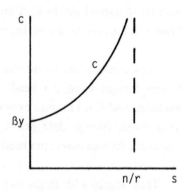

Figure 4
Saving Rate and
Consumption Per Head

We address now the current account. Combine e = nf and (28) to reach:

$$e = \frac{n(s - \alpha n / r)(\alpha / r)^{\alpha/\beta}}{n - rs} \tag{29}$$

If $s \gtrless \alpha n/r$, then $e \gtrless 0$. Put another way, the high-saving country will run a current account surplus. The other way round, the low-saving country will run a current account deficit. Beyond that, a rise in the saving rate boosts the current account surplus per head. Starting from e = 0, an increase in the rate of labour growth reduces the current account surplus per head. And a rise in the foreign interest rate moves up the current account surplus per head.

Another point refers to the trade account. The current account surplus is composed of the trade surplus and the interest inflow e = x + rf. This can be reformulated as e = − q + rf. Here x denotes the trade surplus per head (i.e. net exports per head), and q denotes the trade deficit per head (i.e. net imports per head). In the steady state, it holds e = nf. Compare this with e = − q + rf to derive:

$$q = (r - n)f \tag{30}$$

Finally get rid of f by making use of (28):

$$q = \frac{(r - n)(s - \alpha n / r)(\alpha / r)^{\alpha/\beta}}{n - rs} \tag{31}$$

Let the foreign interest rate exceed the rate of labour growth, which seems to be sound on empirical grounds. Therefore the economy is dynamically efficient. If $s \gtrless \alpha n/r$, then $q \gtrless 0$. As a consequence, the high-saving country will incur a trade deficit. On the other hand, the low-saving country will incur a trade surplus. Owing to (30), a rise in the saving rate enhances the trade deficit per head. Conversely, an increase in the rate of labour growth diminishes the trade deficit per head. And a rise in the foreign interest rate pushes up the trade deficit per head.

What does this mean in terms of capital flows and interest flows? Let s >

$\alpha n/r$, so the country in question will be a creditor. In this case, there is a capital outflow that generates an interest inflow. Strictly speaking, the capital outflow is identical to the current account surplus nf by definition. The interest inflow amounts to rf. From this follows that the interest inflow is greater than the capital outflow rf > nf, due to r > n. The current account surplus per head is nf, while the trade deficit per head is $(r - n)f$. Here two cases can occur. If r > 2n, the trade deficit will be larger than the current account surplus. Yet if r < 2n, the trade deficit will be smaller than the current account surplus.

The natural criterion of efficiency is consumption per head $c = (1 - s)(y + rf)$. A rise in the rate of labour growth depresses foreign assets per head and thus consumption per head. Further throw out f by means of (27) to ascertain:

$$c = \frac{(1-s)\beta ny}{n - rs} \tag{32}$$

For s = 0, we have $c = \beta y > 0$. An increase in the saving rate improves consumption per head, again due to r > n. And as s comes close to n/r, consumption per head tends to explode. Correspondingly figure 4 graphs consumption per head as a function of the saving rate.

Beyond that substitute $y = (\alpha / r)^{\alpha/\beta}$ into (32):

$$c = \frac{(1-s)\beta n(\alpha / r)^{\alpha/\beta}}{n - rs} \tag{33}$$

The evaluation of (33) gives rise to figure 5. Obviously there exists a critical level of the foreign interest rate r'. An increase in the foreign interest rate deteriorates consumption per head, as long as the foreign interest rate stays below the critical level. But as soon as it surpasses this level, the relationship becomes reversed. How does this compare to the closed economy without capital mobility? There the domestic interest rate amounts to $r = \alpha n/s$, as is well known. That is why consumption per head attains only the minimum plotted in figure 5. For the open economy with capital mobility, however, consumption per head lies well above the minimum, whether r < r' or r > r'. As a result, capital mobility increases consumption per head in any case.

For the remainder of this section, we shall give a summary of the conclusions, taking different perspectives. First, a rise in the saving rate does not affect either capital per head or output per head. It raises foreign assets per head. And it lifts consumption per head, provided the foreign interest rate is greater than the rate of labour growth. Second, an increase in the rate of labour growth leaves no impact on capital per head and output per head. It lowers both foreign assets per head and consumption per head. Third, a rise in the foreign interest rate reduces both capital per head and output per head. On the other hand, it pushes up foreign assets per head. When the foreign interest rate is low, it diminishes consumption per head. Conversely, when the foreign interest rate is high, it enhances consumption per head. All of this is in remarkable contrast to the results obtained in the closed economy. Table 1 offers a synopsis.

Table 1
Long-Run Effects (Solow Model)

	s	n	r
k	0	0	−
y	0	0	−
f	+	−	+
e	+	−	+
q	+	−	+
c	+	−	?

The high-saving country makes loans abroad. It holds foreign assets and earns interest on them. The interest inflow allows the country to finance net imports of commodities. The interest inflow gives rise to a current account surplus and a trade deficit. The low-saving country raises loans abroad. It pays interest on foreign debt. In order to finance the interest outflow, the country must be a net exporter of commodities. The interest outflow gives rise to a current account deficit and a trade surplus.

Put another way, the high-saving country will be a creditor. It runs a current account surplus and a trade deficit. An increase in the saving rate moves up foreign assets per head, the current account surplus per head and the trade deficit per head. The low-saving country will be a debtor. It runs a current account deficit and a trade surplus. An increase in the saving rate reduces foreign debt per head, the current account deficit per head and the trade surplus per head.

The fast-growing country will be a debtor. It incurs a current account deficit and a trade surplus. A rise in the rate of labour growth pushes up foreign debt per head, the current account deficit per head and the trade surplus per head. The slow-growing country will be a creditor. It incurs a current account surplus and a trade deficit. A rise in the rate of labour growth pulls down foreign assets per head, the current account surplus per head and the trade deficit per head.

When the foreign interest rate is high, the country in question will be a creditor. It experiences a current account surplus and a trade deficit. A lift in the foreign interest rate boosts foreign assets per head, the current account surplus per head and the trade deficit per head. When the foreign interest rate is low, the country will be a debtor. It experiences a current account deficit and a trade surplus. A lift in the foreign interest rate curtails foreign debt per head, the current account deficit per head and the trade surplus per head.

1.1.2. Process of Adjustment

In this section, we shall study the transitional dynamics of three distinct shocks: an increase in the saving rate, in the rate of labour growth and in the foreign interest rate, respectively. To get ready, solve $\dot{f} = e - nf$ for e and pay attention to $\dot{f} = s(y + rf) - nf - nk$:

$$e = s(y + rf) - nk \tag{1}$$

Accordingly, figure 6 shows the current account surplus per head as a function of foreign assets per head. Besides the diagram contains the nf ray. In the steady state, we have e = nf. In the diagram, the steady state is marked by the point of intersection.

Let us begin with a rise in the saving rate. What will be the effect on foreign assets per head? In the long run, they go up, as is well known. In the short run, however, they do not respond at all. In the diagram, the shock leads to an upward shift in the $s(y + rf) - nk$ line, see figure 7. The short-run equilibrium lies in point 1, the long-run equilibrium in point 2. More precisely, $e = s(y + rf) - nk$ is the actual current account surplus per head. nf, by way of contrast, is the current account surplus per head that is required to keep foreign assets per head constant. In the short run, the current account surplus per head exceeds the required level, hence foreign assets per head are adjusted upwards. For the associated time path see figure 8.

Next have a look at consumption per head. In the long run, an increase in the saving rate raises consumption per head. In the short run, by virtue of $c = (1 - s)(y + rf)$, an increase in the saving rate lowers consumption per head. Putting all pieces of the puzzle together, figure 9 presents the time path of consumption per head. What about the current account? The model has it that $e = s(y + rf) - nk$. At first, a rise in the saving rate augments the current account surplus per head. Later on, as foreign assets per head are piled up, the current account surplus per head continues to swell. The time path can be found in figure 10. At last a few words will be said on the trade account. In the long run, an increase in the saving

26

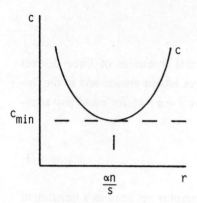

Figure 5
Foreign Interest Rate and
Consumption Per Head

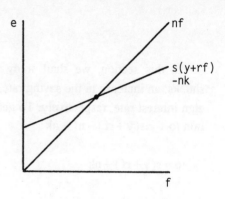

Figure 6
Current Account Surplus Per Head

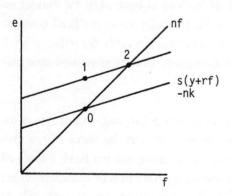

Figure 7
Increase in Saving Rate

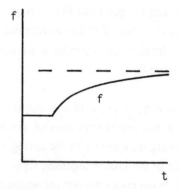

Figure 8
Foreign Assets Per Head

rate drives up the trade deficit per head. In the short run, the argument goes as follows. Equate $e = -q + rf$ and $e = s(y + rf) - nk$ to get:

$$q = rf + nk - s(y + rf) \tag{2}$$

In the short run, therefore, an increase in the saving rate reduces the trade deficit per head. For the time path see figure 11.

After having completed these preparatory tasks, we shall give a causal interpretation of the process of adjustment set in motion by an increase in the saving rate. Initially the economy is in the steady state. The current account surplus per head and foreign assets per head do not change. Likewise investment per head, capital per head and output per head are invariant. And the same is true of consumption per head and net imports per head. Against this background, the saving rate is boosted. In the short run, this depresses consumption per head. Accordingly, net imports per head come down and the current account surplus per head goes up. Investment per head, however, stays put.

In the medium run, the rise in the current account surplus per head contributes to the accumulation of foreign assets per head. Capital per head and output per head are still at rest, since investment per head did not respond. Moreover, due to the accumulation of foreign assets per head, the interest inflow per head expands, thereby improving the income per head of domestic residents and hence consumption per head. The recovery of consumption per head goes along with a recovery of net imports per head. And the expansion of the interest inflow per head leads to an expansion of the current account surplus per head.

As time proceeds, the economy approaches a new steady state. The current account surplus per head and foreign assets per head have stopped to adjust. As always, investment per head, capital per head and output per head are uniform. Consumption per head and net imports per head do no longer change. Taking the sum over the process of adjustment as a whole, the current account surplus per head and foreign assets per head went up. Investment per head, capital per head and output per head did not react at all. Consumption per head and net imports per head rose.

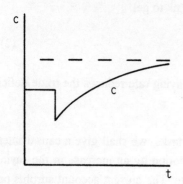

Figure 9
Consumption Per Head

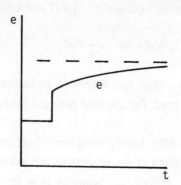

Figure 10
Current Account Surplus Per Head

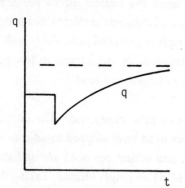

Figure 11
Trade Deficit Per Head

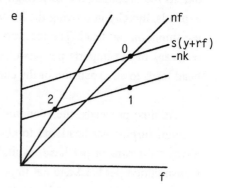

Figure 12
Increase in Labour Growth

Here a comment is in place on the underlying export function. The part of domestic output that is neither consumed nor invested at home, will be exported. As far as the import function is concerned, it goes the other way round. The part of domestic consumption and investment that is not produced at home, will be imported.

At this point, we leave the saving shock and turn to the labour growth shock. In the long run, a rise in the rate of labour growth diminishes foreign assets per head. Yet in the short run, the shock leaves no impact on foreign assets per head. In figure 12, the disturbance shifts the $s(y + rf) - nk$ line downwards and rotates the nf ray counter-clockwise. 0 indicates the pre-shock steady state, 1 the momentary equilibrium after shock, and 2 the post-shock steady state. In the momentary equilibrium, the current account surplus per head falls short of the required level, so foreign assets per head decline. Figure 13 illustrates how foreign assets per head travel through time.

What does this imply for consumption per head? In the long run, an increase in the rate of labour growth cuts back consumption per head. In the short run, owing to $c = (1 - s)(y + rf)$, consumption per head remains unchanged. Figure 14 portrays the resulting time path. Beyond that verify the current account. In the model we have $e = s(y + rf) - nk$. At first, a rise in the rate of labour growth contracts the current account surplus per head. Later on, as foreign assets per head drop, the current account surplus per head keeps on skrinking. From figure 15 one can learn how the current account develops. At last review the trade account. In the long run, an increase in the rate of labour growth depresses net imports per head. In the short run, thanks to $q = rf + nk - s(y + rf)$, net imports per head surge. The time path can be found in figure 16.

Next we shall trace out the transitional dynamics of a labour growth shock. At the beginning the economy is in the steady state. The current account surplus per head and foreign assets per head are constant. Investment, capital and output, in per capita terms respectively, do not vary. The same applies to consumption and net imports. Then the rate of labour growth springs up on its own. In the short run, this enlarges investment per head. For that reason, net imports per head mount and the current account surplus per head descends. Consumption per head does not stir.

30

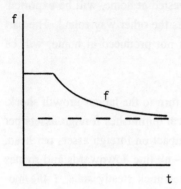

Figure 13
Foreign Assets Per Head

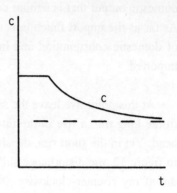

Figure 14
Consumption Per Head

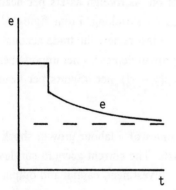

Figure 15
Current Account Surplus Per Head

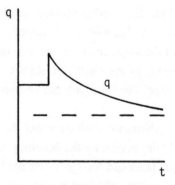

Figure 16
Trade Deficit Per Head

In the medium run, the fall in the current account surplus per head lowers foreign assets per head. Capital per head and output per head are invariant. In addition, because of the decumulation of foreign assets per head, the interest inflow per head lessens, thus restraining the income per head of domestic residents and their consumption per head. The cutback in consumption per head is accompanied by a cutback in net imports per head. And the lessening of the interest inflow per head brings about a decline of the current account surplus per head. Asymptotically, the economy reaches a new steady state. The current account surplus per head and foreign assets per head come to a standstill. Investment, capital and output, in per capita terms, are still unaffected. Consumption per head and net imports per head do no longer move.

Third have a look at an increase in the foreign interest rate. In the long run, this raises foreign assets per head. In the short run, this lowers capital per head, thereby raising foreign assets per head as well. Does this mean that foreign assets per head overshoot in the short run? To answer this question, consider a numerical example with $\alpha = 0.2$, $n = 0.03$, $r = 0.06$ and $s = 0.1$. At the start let the economy be in the steady state $k = (\alpha / r)^{1/\beta} = 4.5040$, $y = (\alpha / r)^{\alpha/\beta} = 1.3512$ and $f = (sy - nk)/(n - rs) = 0$. Now let the foreign interest rate spring up from 0.06 to 0.07. At once this reduces capital per head to 3.7146 and output per head to 1.3001. Thus, in the short run, capital per head falls by 0.7894. Of course, foreign assets per head rise by the same amount, i.e. they are 0.7894. In the long run, foreign assets per head keep on rising to 0.8075. As a consequence, there is no overshooting. In figure 17, the increase in the foreign interest rate shifts the $s(y + rf) - nk$ line upwards. The long-run equilibria can be read off, as well as the short-run equilibrium. Correspondingly, figure 18 displays the time path of foreign assets per head.

Next regard consumption per head $c = (1 - s)(y + rf)$, drawing again on the numerical example. In the initial steady state, we have $c = 1.2160$. Then the foreign interest rate climbs. In the short run, this brings up consumption per head to 1.2198. In the long run, consumption per head continues to grow to 1.2210. Figure 19 illustrates the dynamics of consumption per head. What about the current account surplus per head $e = s(y + rf) - nk$? As a point of departure, we get $e = 0$. Then the foreign interest rate is driven up. Instantaneously, therefore, capital per head drops by 0.7894. This, in turn, is equivalent to a current account surplus per head of 0.7894. In the short run, the current account surplus per head is cut back

32

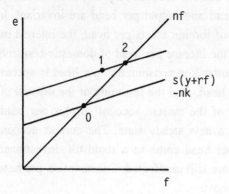

Figure 17
Increase in Foreign Interest Rate

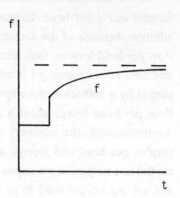

Figure 18
Foreign Assets Per Head

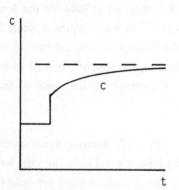

Figure 19
Consumption Per Head

to 0.0241, in the long run it is stepped up a bit to 0.0242. Figure 20 plots the transition. Further contemplate the trade deficit per head $q = rf + nk - s(y + rf)$. As a starting point, we have $q = 0$. Then the economy is hit by the shock. At once this reduces capital per head by 0.7894. Evidently, this amounts to a trade surplus per head of 0.7894. In the short run, the trade surplus per head is $- 0.0312$, in the long run it is $- 0.0323$. For the time path see figure 21.

At last we shall present the process of adjustment coherently. At the beginning the economy is in the steady state. The current account surplus per head and foreign assets per head do not move. Investment per head, capital per head and output per head are uniform. The same is valid of consumption per head and the trade deficit per head. In these circumstances, the foreign interest rate goes up. Instantaneously, in order to equate the marginal product of capital to the foreign interest rate, capital flows out. Properly speaking, there is a decline in capital per head that causes an increase in foreign assets per head. In the medium run, foreign assets per head are piled up round by round. Capital per head and output per head are again invariant. The net effect is that consumption per head, the trade deficit per head and the current account surplus per head expand. In due course, the economy tends to a new steady state. The current account surplus per head and foreign assets per head do not move any longer. Investment per head, capital per head and output per head are uniform. The same applies to consumption per head and the trade deficit per head.

1.2. Foreign Debt

In the preceding section, emphasis was laid on foreign assets. In the current section, instead, it will be placed on foreign debt. Domestic output and net imports can be dedicated to consumption and investment $Y + Q = C + I$. Now a few words will be said on the dynamics of foreign debt. Domestic residents pay the interest rate r on foreign debt D, so the interest outflow amounts to rD. The income of domestic residents equals factor income diminished by the interest outflow $Y - rD$. Households put aside a given part of their income for saving purpo-

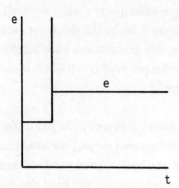

Figure 20
Current Account Surplus Per Head

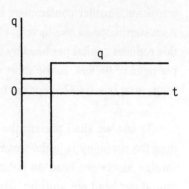

Figure 21
Trade Deficit Per Head

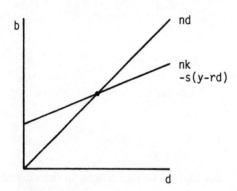

Figure 22
Current Account Deficit Per Head

ses S = s(Y − rD) with s = const. The income of domestic residents can be used for consumption and savings Y − rD = C + S. This yields the consumption function C = (1 − s)(Y − rD). The current account deficit is defined as the sum of net imports and the interest outflow B = Q + rD. The current account deficit in turn adds to foreign debt $\dot{D}$ = B.

In full analogy to the preceding section, the model can be described by a system of eight equations:

$$Y = K^{\alpha}N^{\beta} \tag{1}$$

$$r = \alpha Y / K \tag{2}$$

$$Y = C + I - Q \tag{3}$$

$$C = (1 - s)(Y - rD) \tag{4}$$

$$I = nK \tag{5}$$

$$B = Q + rD \tag{6}$$

$$\dot{D} = B \tag{7}$$

$$\dot{N} = nN \tag{8}$$

Here α, β, n, r, s, D and N are exogenous, while B, C, $\dot{D}$, I, K, $\dot{N}$, X and Y are endogenous.

Now the model will be transformed into per capita terms. y = c + i − q takes the place of Y = C + I − Q, where q = Q/N stands for net imports per head. The consumption function is c = (1 − s)(y − rd), with foreign debt per head d = D/N. The current account equation is b = q + rd, with current account deficit per head b = B/N. Moreover take the time derivative of foreign debt per head $\dot{d} = \dot{D}/N - D\dot{N}/N^2$ and note $\dot{D}$ = B to conclude $\dot{d} = b - nd$.

In per capita terms, the model can be written as a system of seven equations:

$$y = k^{\alpha} \tag{9}$$

$$r = \alpha y / k \tag{10}$$

$$y = c + i - q \tag{11}$$

$$c = (1-s)(y-rd) \tag{12}$$

$$i = nk \tag{13}$$

$$b = q + rd \tag{14}$$

$$\dot{d} = b - nd \tag{15}$$

Here α, d, n, r and s are given, whereas b, c, $\dot{d}$, i, k, q and y adjust themselves.

In addition, insert (12) as well as (13) into (11) and solve for $q = (1 - s)(y - rd) + nk - y$. Then put this into (14) to verify:

$$b = nk - s(y - rd) \tag{16}$$

Further eliminate b in (15) with the help of (16):

$$\dot{d} = nk - s(y - rd) - nd \tag{17}$$

In the steady state, the motion of foreign debt per head comes to a standstill $\dot{d} = 0$. Combine this with (17) to find out the equilibrium value:

$$d = \frac{nk - sy}{n - rs} \tag{18}$$

By the way, can it happen that the income of domestic residents becomes negative? Substitute (18) into $y - rd$ and rearrange to ascertain $y - rd = \beta ny/(n - rs)$. Due to $n > rs$, this will always be positive.

Along the same lines as before, the following results can be obtained. An increase in the saving rate does affect neither capital per head nor output per head. It reduces foreign debt per head. And it improves consumption per head, provided $r > n$. An increase in the rate of labour growth leaves no impact on capital per head and output per head. It increases foreign debt per head and worsens consumption per head. An increase in the foreign interest rate depresses both capital per head and output per head. Besides it brings down foreign debt per head. As long as the foreign interest rate is low, the shock deteriorates consumption per head. But as soon as the foreign interest rate is sufficiently high, the shock improves consumption per head. Table 2 presents an overview of these effects.

Table 2
Long-Run Effects (Solow Model)

	s	n	r
k	0	0	–
y	0	0	–
d	–	+	–
b	–	+	–
x	–	+	–
c	+	–	?

For the rest of this section, we shall keep track of the process of adjustment. Figure 22 shows the current account deficit per head as a function of foreign debt per head $b = nk - s(y - rd)$. Beyond that it contains the nd ray. In the steady state, it holds $b = nd$. In the diagram, the steady state is marked by the crossing point. Now have a look at an increase in the saving rate. In figure 23, this shifts the $nk - s(y - rd)$ line downwards. More exactly, $b = nk - s(y - rd)$ symbolizes the actual current account deficit per head. nd, on the other hand, is the current account deficit per head that is required to keep foreign debt per head constant. In the short-run position 1, the current account deficit per head lies well below the required level, so foreign debt per head declines. Figure 24 depicts the time pattern of foreign debt per head.

What does this imply for the current account deficit per head? The model has it that $b = nk - s(y - rd)$. At first, the increase in the saving rate cuts back the current account deficit per head. Later on, the decline in foreign debt per head cuts back the current account deficit per head even further. Figure 25 illustrates how

38

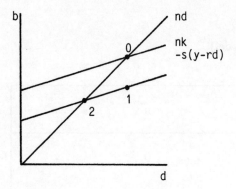

Figure 23
Increase in Saving Rate

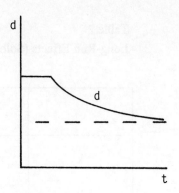

Figure 24
Foreign Debt Per Head

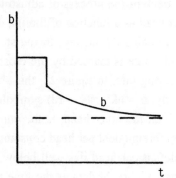

Figure 25
Current Account Deficit Per Head

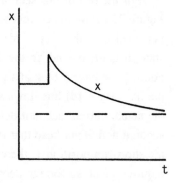

Figure 26
Trade Surplus Per Head

the current account deficit moves over time. What about the trade surplus per head? In the long run, an increase in the saving rate puts downward pressure on the trade surplus per head. In the short run, we have $q = rf + nk - s(y + rf)$, which can be restated as:

$$x = s(y - rd) + rd - nk \tag{19}$$

Therefore, in the short run, an increase in the saving rate puts upward pressure on the trade surplus per head. For the trajectory see figure 26.

Next transitional dynamics will be set forth in greater detail. At the start, let the economy be in the steady state. The current account deficit per head and foreign debt per head do not change. Investment per head, capital per head and output per head are invariant. The same is valid of consumption per head and net exports per head. Against this background, the saving rate is driven up. In the short run, this lowers consumption per head. The ensuing rise in net exports per head induces a fall in the current account deficit per head. Investment per head, however, stays put.

In the medium run, the fall in the current account deficit per head contributes to the decumulation of foreign debt per head. Capital per head and output per head do not vary, since investment per head stayed put. Owing to the decumulation of foreign debt per head, the interest outflow per head lessens, which raises the income per head of domestic residents and hence their consumption per head. The rise in consumption per head in turn causes a fall in net exports per head. And the lessening of the interest outflow per head decreases the current account deficit per head.

As time goes on, the economy approximates a new steady state. The current account deficit per head and foreign debt per head do no longer change. The same is valid of consumption per head and net exports per head. Over the process of adjustment as a whole, the current account deficit per head and foreign debt per head drop. Consumption per head climbs, while net exports per head drop.

1.3. Assets

Let us set out with asset dynamics. Domestic residents earn the interest rate r on assets A, so asset income amounts to rA. The income of domestic residents is composed of labour income and asset income wN + rA. Together with wN = βY, this can be written as βY + rA. Households save a certain fraction of their income S = s(βY + rA) with s = const. Savings, in turn, contribute to the accumulation of assets $\dot{A}$ = S. In this way, the model can be characterized by a system of four equations:

$$Y = K^{\alpha} N^{\beta} \tag{1}$$

$$r = \alpha Y / K \tag{2}$$

$$\dot{A} = s(\beta Y + rA) \tag{3}$$

$$\dot{N} = nN \tag{4}$$

Here α, β, n, r, s, A and N are exogenous, whereas $\dot{A}$, K, $\dot{N}$ and Y are endogenous.

At this point we switch to per capita terms. a = A/N symbolizes assets per head. Now take the time derivative of assets per head $\dot{a} = \dot{A} / N - A\dot{N} / N^2$. Then observe $\dot{A} = s(\beta Y + rA)$ to attain $\dot{a} = s(\beta y + ra) - na$. Thus the model can be reformulated as a system of three equations:

$$y = k^{\alpha} \tag{5}$$

$$r = \alpha y / k \tag{6}$$

$$\dot{a} = s(\beta y + ra) - na \tag{7}$$

Here α, a, n, r and s are fixed, while $\dot{a}$, k and y are flexible.

In the steady state, the movement of assets per head grinds to a halt $\dot{a} = 0$. Therefore the steady state can be decribed by:

$$y = k^\alpha \tag{8}$$

$$r = \alpha y / k \tag{9}$$

$$na = s(\beta y + ra) \tag{10}$$

Here α, n, r and s are given, whereas a, k and y adjust themselves. Further check stability. Differentiate (7) for a to find out:

$$\frac{d\dot{a}}{da} = rs - n < 0 \tag{11}$$

Hence the steady state proves to be stable.

Next we shall make a few comments on the steady state. To begin with, solve (10) for:

$$a = \frac{\beta sy}{n - rs} \tag{12}$$

Then take account of $y = (\alpha / r)^{\alpha/\beta}$:

$$a = \frac{\beta s(\alpha / r)^{\alpha/\beta}}{n - rs} \tag{13}$$

For s = 0, we have a = 0. What is more, an increase in the saving rate pushes up assets per head. As s approaches n/r from below, a tends to infinity. Conversely, an increase in the rate of labour growth pulls down assets per head. Besides figure 27 plots assets per head as a function of the foreign interest rate. Obviously, there exists a critical level of the foreign interest rate r'. When r < r', then an increase in the foreign interest rate lowers assets per head. On the other hand, when r > r', then an increase in the foreign interest rate raises assets per head.

At last we shed some light on transitional dynamics. Figure 28 portrays savings per head as a function of assets per head s(βy + ra). Beyond that it depicts the na ray. The steady state is situated in the point of intersection. Now consider an increase in the saving rate. In figure 29, the shock displaces the s(βy + ra) line upwards. Strictly speaking, s(βy + ra) denotes actual savings per head. na, however, indicates the savings per head that are required to keep assets per head con-

42

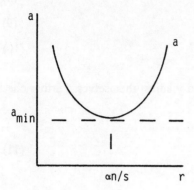

Figure 27
Foreign Interest Rate
and Assets Per Head

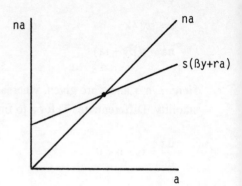

Figure 28
Savings Per Head

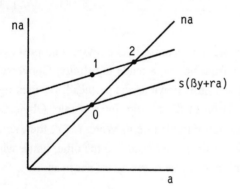

Figure 29
Increase in Saving Rate

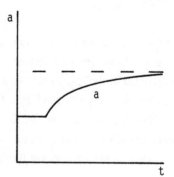

Figure 30
Assets Per Head

stant. In the temporary equilibrium 1, savings per head lie well above the required level, so assets per head are heaped up. Figure 30 demonstrates the time path of assets per head.

Coming to an end, we discuss the process of adjustment more closely. Initially, the economy is in the steady state. Savings per head and assets per head are uniform. Then all of a sudden the saving rate jumps up. In the short run, this lifts savings per head. In the medium run, due to the rise in savings per head, assets per head grow period by period. Asymptotically, the economy reaches a new steady. Savings per head and assets per head are again uniform.

1.4. Numerical Example

So far we took the per head approach, now we shall change to the ratio approach. Consider for instance the capital-output ratio instead of capital per head. With this new method, results are more elegant and appeal more to intuition (as far as the order of magnitude is concerned, in the numerical example).

As a starting point, take the steady state derived in section 1.1.1.:

$$y = k^\alpha \tag{1}$$

$$r = \alpha y / k \tag{2}$$

$$y = c + i + x \tag{3}$$

$$c = (1 - s)(y + rf) \tag{4}$$

$$i = nk \tag{5}$$

$$e = x + rf \tag{6}$$

$$nf = e \tag{7}$$

Here α, n, r and s are exogenous, while c, e, f, i, k, x and y are endogenous.

44

Let us begin with the capital-output ratio. Compare its definition $v = k/y$ with $r = \alpha y/k$ to get:

$$v = \alpha / r \tag{8}$$

The next point refers to the foreign asset ratio, i.e. the share of foreign assets in domestic output (income). Combine $f = (sy - nk)/(n - rs)$ as well as $r = \alpha y/k$ and rearrange:

$$\frac{f}{y} = \frac{s - \alpha n / r}{n - rs} \tag{9}$$

This is the equation of the foreign asset ratio. Further have a look at the current account surplus ratio, i.e. the share of the current account surplus in domestic output. Substitute (9) into $e = nf$ to gain:

$$\frac{e}{y} = \frac{ns - \alpha n^2 / r}{n - rs} \tag{10}$$

This is the current account surplus ratio. Likewise contemplate the trade deficit ratio, i.e. the share of the trade deficit in domestic output. Eliminate f in $q = (r - n)f$ by means of (9) and reshuffle:

$$\frac{q}{y} = \frac{(r - n)(s - \alpha n / r)}{n - rs} \tag{11}$$

This is the trade deficit ratio. Similarly, the interest inflow ratio denotes the share of the interest inflow in domestic output.

The numerical example is based on the parameter values $\alpha = 0.2$, $\beta = 0.8$, $n = 0.03$, $r = 0.06$ and $s = 0.1$. In a sense, n includes both the rate of population growth (e.g. 0.01) and the rate of technical progress (e.g. 0.02). As a consequence, we find $f/y = e/y = q/y = rf/y = 0$. That means, the foreign position, the current account and the trade account are balanced. In addition, there is no interest flow. Of course, the parameters have been chosen so as to get this result. Besides, consumption per head amounts to 1.22. See table 3 for a synopsis.

Table 3
Different Saving Rates

s	f/y	e/y	q/y	rf/y	c
0	- 3.33	- 0.10	- 0.10	- 0.20	1.08
0.06	- 1.52	- 0.05	- 0.05	- 0.09	1.15
0.08	- 0.79	- 0.02	- 0.02	- 0.05	1.18
0.09	- 0.41	- 0.01	- 0.01	- 0.02	1.20
0.10	0	0	0	0	1.22
0.11	0.43	0.01	0.01	0.03	1.23
0.12	0.88	0.03	0.03	0.05	1.25
0.14	1.85	0.06	0.06	0.11	1.29
0.20	5.56	0.17	0.17	0.33	1.44

First regard an increase in the saving rate from 0.10 to 0.11. This yields f/y = 0.43, e/y = 0.013, q/y = 0.013 and rf/y = 0.026. Put another way, foreign assets are 43% of output, the current account surplus is 1.3%, the trade deficit is 1.3% and the interest inflow is 2.6%. Consumption per head rises from 1.22 to 1.23. Beyond that, imagine a further increase in the saving rate from 0.11 to 0.12. For that reason, foreign assets go up from 43% to 88%, nearly doubling. The current account surplus is lifted from 1.3% to 2.6%, and the same applies to the trade deficit. The interest inflow swells from 2.6% to 5.3%. Consumption per head is raised from 1.23 to 1.25.

Having done this, let us return to the baseline s = 0.10, which involves f/y = e/y = q/y = rf/y = 0. Now consider a reduction in the saving rate from 0.10 to 0.09. Accordingly, one calculates f/y = − 0.41, e/y = − 0.012, q/y = − 0.012 and rf/y = − 0.024. In other words, foreign debt is 41% of output, the current account deficit is 1.2%, the trade surplus is 1.2% and the interest outflow is 2.4%. Consumption per head falls from 1.22 to 1.20. In a second step, let the saving rate

46

drop from 0.09 to 0.08. On these grounds, foreign debt is driven up from 41% to 79%. The current account deficit climbs from 1.2% to 2.4%, the same holding of the trade surplus. The interest outflow, too, becomes broader (from 2.4% to 4.8%). Consumption per head is cut back from 1.20 to 1.18.

So much for variations in the saving rate, we come next to variations in the foreign interest rate. Suppose again $\alpha = 0.2$, $n = 0.03$, $r = 0.06$ and $s = 0.1$. From this one can infer $v = 3.3$ and $f/y = e/y = 0$. That is to say, the foreign position and the current account are balanced. Table 4 presents an overview. First examine an increase in the foreign interest rate from 0.06 to 0.07. As an effect, this lowers the capital-output ratio from 3.3 to 2.9. The country in question becomes a creditor and runs a current account surplus. Foreign assets are 62%, and the current account surplus is 1.9%. The other way round, assume a reduction in the foreign interest rate from 0.06 to 0.05. This raises the capital-output ratio from 3.3 to 4.0. The country becomes a debtor and incurs a current account deficit. Foreign debt is 80%, and the current account deficit is 2.4%.

Table 4
Different Interest Rates

r	v	f/y	e/y
0.05	4.0	- 0.80	- 0.02
0.06	3.3	0	0
0.07	2.9	+ 0.62	+ 0.02

In full analogy, we investigate shocks in the rate of labour growth. Let us start again from the premise $\alpha = 0.2$, $n = 0.03$, $r = 0.06$ and $s = 0.1$. This produces $f/y = e/y = 0$. For a summary catch a glimpse of table 5. Now postulate an increase in the rate of labour growth from 0.03 to 0.04. That is why the country in question becomes a debtor and runs a current account deficit. Foreign debt is

98%, and the current account deficit is 3.9%. Conversely take a reduction in the rate of labour growth from 0.03 to 0.02. The country becomes a creditor and incurs a current account surplus. Foreign assets are 238%, and the current account surplus is 4.8%.

Table 5
Different Growth Rates

n	f/y	e/y
0.02	2.4	0.05
0.03	0	0
0.04	- 1.0	- 0.04

To sum up, in the model, a small change in the saving rate causes a very big change in the foreign asset ratio. This, however, seems not to be consistent with empirical evidence. In advanced countries, foreign asset ratios appear to be rather low, in spite of the fact that saving rates differ among countries quite a lot. In Germany, for instance, foreign assets reached a maximum of about 20 percent of GDP. In the United States, for that matter, foreign debt is near 10 percent of GDP. This suggests that, in the real world, capital mobility is more or less imperfect, see chapter III below.

So far, capital mobility was assumed to be given. Now we shall study the effects of introducing capital mobility. Properly speaking, we shall compare the steady state with capital mobility to that without capital mobility. In the steady state without capital mobility, we have $k = (s/n)^{1/\beta}$, $y = (s/n)^{\alpha/\beta}$, $c = (1-s)y$ and $r = \alpha y/k$, as is well known. As a result, table 6 displays the steady state without capital mobility, taking account of a broad range of saving rates. Correspondingly, table 7 presents the steady state with capital mobility. Then the comparative evaluation of tables 6 and 7 yields the long-run consequences of introducing capital mobility, cf. table 8.

Table 6
Steady State without Capital Mobility

s	k	y	c	r
0	0	0	0	∞
0.06	2.38	1.19	1.12	0.100
0.08	3.41	1.28	1.18	0.075
0.09	3.95	1.32	1.20	0.067
0.10	4.50	1.35	1.22	0.060
0.11	5.07	1.38	1.23	0.055
0.12	5.66	1.41	1.24	0.050
0.14	6.86	1.47	1.26	0.043
0.20	10.71	1.61	1.29	0.030

At first consider a saving rate of 6%. In the steady state without capital mobility, capital per head is 2.38, and output per head is 1.19. Of course, the foreign position is balanced d = 0. Consumption per head is 1.12, and the interest rate is 0.100. In the steady state with capital mobility, on the other hand, capital per head is 4.50, and output per head is 1.35. Foreign debt per head amounts to 2.05, so the foreign debt ratio equals 1.52. Consumption per head is 1.15, and the interest rate is 0.060. That means, capital mobility increases capital per head by 89%. The foreign debt ratio rises from 0% to 152%. And consumption per head goes up by 3.3%.

Table 7

Steady State with Capital Mobility

s	k	y	f	c
0	4.50	1.35	- 4.50	1.08
0.06	4.50	1.35	- 2.05	1.15
0.08	4.50	1.35	- 1.07	1.18
0.09	4.50	1.35	- 0.55	1.20
0.10	4.50	1.35	0	1.22
0.11	4.50	1.35	+ 0.58	1.23
0.12	4.50	1.35	+ 1.19	1.25
0.14	4.50	1.35	+ 2.50	1.29
0.20	4.50	1.35	+ 7.51	1.44

Instead, have a look at a saving rate of 14%. In the steady state without capital mobility, capital per head is 6.86, and output per head is 1.47. There are no foreign assets $f = 0$. Consumption per head is 1.26, and the interest rate is 0.043. In the steady state with capital mobility, as opposed to that, capital per head is again 4.50, and output per head is 1.35. Foreign assets per head reach 2.50, thus the foreign asset ratio equals 1.85. Consumption per head is 1.29, and the interest rate is again 0.060. In other words, capital mobility reduces capital per head by 34%. Conversely, the foreign asset ratio jumps up from 0% to 185%. On these grounds, consumption per head improves by 2.1%. For a more detailed analysis, see the two-country Solow model with different saving rates (chapter II, section 2).

Table 8
Introducing Capital Mobility

s	k	c
0	$+\infty\%$	$+\infty\%$
0.06	$+89\%$	$+3.3\%$
0.08	$+32\%$	$+0.7\%$
0.09	$+14\%$	$+0.2\%$
0.10	0%	0.0%
0.11	-11%	$+0.1\%$
0.12	-20%	$+0.6\%$
0.14	-34%	$+2.1\%$
0.20	-58%	$+12.1\%$

The last (and separate) point of this section refers to the dynamics of the special case n = rs. Initially let the economy be in a steady state with $\alpha = 0.2$, n = 0.03, r = 0.06 and s = 0.1. Therefore the foreign asset ratio is zero. Against this background, the rate of labour growth falls from 0.03 to 0.006, which is the critical level n = rs. Then the foreign asset ratio moves according to the law:

$$\frac{f_{+1}}{y} = \frac{f}{y} + s(1+\frac{rf}{y}) - \frac{nf}{y} - \frac{nk}{y} \tag{12}$$

In period 1, the foreign asset ratio climbs to 0.08, in period 2 to 0.16, in period 3 to 0.24, and so on. As a finding, due to the shock, the foreign asset ratio tends to infinity. Put another way, there exists no steady state. By virtue of a = f + k and c = (1 − s)(y + rf), the asset ratio a/y and consumption per head grow without limits, too.

1.5. Delayed Adjustment of Capital Stock

In the preceding sections, we supposed that the capital stock adjusts instantaneously. In the current section, as an alternative, we postulate that the capital stock adjusts only slowly. This can be attributed to the cost of adjustment. That is to say, investment serves to fill the gap between the desired and the actual stock of capital step by step. More exactly, if desired capital per head $k^* = \alpha y/r$ exceeds actual capital per head k, then actual capital per head rises $\dot{k} = \lambda(\alpha y/r - k)$, where $\lambda > 0$ denotes the speed of adjustment. In addition, the increase in assets depends on savings $\dot{F} + \dot{K} = s(Y + rF)$, which can be reformulated in per capita terms as $\dot{f} + \dot{k} = s(y + rf) - nf - nk$.

In a nutshell, the model can be represented by a system of three equations:

$$y = k^\alpha \tag{1}$$

$$\dot{k} = \lambda(\alpha y/r - k) \tag{2}$$

$$\dot{f} + \dot{k} = s(y + rf) - nf - nk \tag{3}$$

Here α, λ, f, k, n, r and s are exogenous, while $\dot{f}$, $\dot{k}$ and y are endogenous.

In the steady state, both foreign assets per head and capital per head do not move any longer $\dot{f} = \dot{k} = 0$. For that reason, the steady state can be written down as follows:

$$y = k^\alpha \tag{4}$$

$$r = \alpha y/k \tag{5}$$

$$nf + nk = s(y + rf) \tag{6}$$

In this situation, α, n, r and s are given, whereas f, k and y adjust themselves. Obviously the steady state with delayed adjustment is identical to the steady state with instantaneous adjustment.

Next we shall discuss stability by adopting phase diagram techniques. The model can be further compressed to a system of two differential equations:

$$\dot{f} = g(f,k) \tag{7}$$
$$\dot{k} = h(f,k) \tag{8}$$

Let us begin with $\dot{k}$. (1) and (2) can be combined to give:

$$\dot{k} = \lambda(\alpha k^{\alpha} / r - k) \tag{9}$$

Now differentiate (9) for k and evaluate the derivative at the steady state with $r = \alpha k^{-\beta}$ to ascertain:

$$\frac{\partial \dot{k}}{\partial k} = -\beta \lambda < 0 \tag{10}$$

Then set (9) equal to zero and solve for k:

$$k = (\alpha / r)^{1/\beta} \tag{11}$$

Hence k is independent of f. Correspondingly, figure 31 shows the horizontal $\dot{k} = 0$ demarcation line.

Let us turn to $\dot{f}$. From (1), (2) and (3), one can deduce:

$$\dot{f} = s(k^{\alpha} + rf) - nf - nk - \lambda(\alpha k^{\alpha} / r - k) \tag{12}$$

Differentiate (12) for f to verify:

$$\frac{\partial \dot{f}}{\partial f} = rs - n < 0 \tag{13}$$

Besides set (12) equal to zero, which yields:

$$(n - rs)f = (\lambda - n)k - (\alpha \lambda / r - s)k^{\alpha} \tag{14}$$

We posit $n > rs$, $s < \alpha\lambda/r$ as well as $\lambda > n$, thus the terms in brackets are positive. Accordingly, figure 31 visualizes the backward bending $\dot{f} = 0$ demarcation line. The lesson taught by the directional arrows is that the steady state is stable. In the phase diagram, foreign assets per head can be either positive or negative.

For the remainder of this section, we shall keep track of the process of adjustment set in motion by a lift in the foreign interest rate. Owing to (11), the $\dot{k} = 0$ line is shifted downwards, see figure 32. And by virtue of (14), the $\dot{f} = 0$ line goes to the right. In figure 32, the streamline indicates how the economy travels through time. Figure 33 plots the delayed adjustment of capital per head 1. As a base of comparison, it also contains the instantaneous adjustment of capital per head 2. Similarly, figure 34 depicts the time path of foreign assets per head.

Finally we shall give a causal interpretation of dynamics. At the start, the economy is in the steady state. The current account surplus per head and foreign assets per head are constant. Investment per head and capital per head do not change. Then, abruptly, the foreign interest rate shoots up. In the short run, this raises the interest inflow per head and thereby the current account surplus per head. On the other hand, the shock lowers desired capital per head and so investment per head. In the medium run, the rise in the current account surplus per head contributes to the accumulation of foreign assets per head. By way of contrast, the fall in investment per head leads to the decumulation of capital per head. As time passes away, the economy approaches a new steady state. The current account surplus per head and foreign assets per head are again invariant. Investment per head and capital per head have stopped to adjust. In summary, foreign assets per head settle at a higher level, while capital per head has been run down.

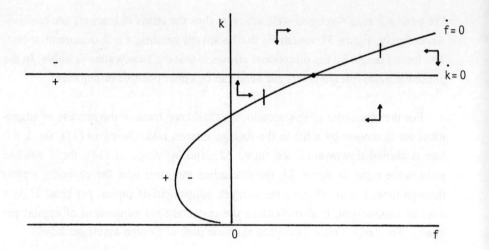

Figure 31
Delayed Adjustment

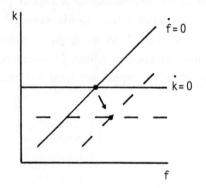

Figure 32
Increase in Foreign Interest Rate

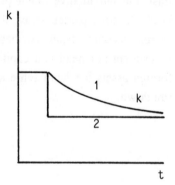

Figure 33
Capital Per Head

1.6. Technical Progress at Home

At first consider a one-time technical progress. The model can be described by a system of three equations:

$$y = \varepsilon k^{\alpha} \tag{1}$$
$$r = \alpha y / k \tag{2}$$
$$\dot{f} = s(y + rf) - nf - nk \tag{3}$$

(1) is the production function in per capita terms, where ε symbolizes efficiency. (2) has it that the foreign interest rate equals the marginal product of capital. And according to (3), the current account surplus adds to foreign assets. Here α, ε, f, n, r and s are fixed, while $\dot{f}$, k and y are flexible.

From (1) and (2) one can infer:

$$k = \varepsilon^{1/\beta} (\alpha / r)^{1/\beta} \tag{4}$$
$$y = \varepsilon^{1/\beta} (\alpha / r)^{\alpha/\beta} \tag{5}$$

That is to say, an increase in efficiency raises both capital per head and output per head. Before shock, the marginal product of capital coincides with the foreign interest rate. Then the increase in efficiency drives up the marginal product of capital well above the foreign interest rate. Therefore, at once, capital flows in. That means, capital per head rises, thus lowering the marginal product of capital. After shock, the marginal product of capital corresponds again to the foreign interest rate.

Now take a look at the steady state. Along the same lines as in the preceding sections, foreign assets per head can be stated as f = (s − αn/r)y/(n − rs) (cf. section 1.4., equation (9)). Further eliminate y with the help of (5) to get:

$$f = \frac{(s - \alpha n / r)\varepsilon^{1/\beta} (\alpha / r)^{\alpha/\beta}}{n - rs} \tag{6}$$

As a consequence, the high-saving country will be a creditor. And an increase in efficiency pushes up foreign assets per head. The other way round, the low-saving country will be a debtor. In these circumstances, an increase in efficiency pushes up foreign debt per head. This is in remarkable contrast to a lift in the saving rate, which either expands foreign assets per head or contracts foreign debt per head.

Next we shall trace out the dynamics kicked off by a one-time technical progress. In figure 35, the s(y + rf) − nk line portrays the actual current account surplus per head, and the nf ray graphs the required current account surplus per head. At the beginning, the economy is in the steady state. Foreign assets per head do not move. In the diagram, this is marked by 0. All of a sudden, there occurs an increase in efficiency. In the short run, this induces a capital inflow. Capital per head rises, while foreign assets per head fall. In the diagram, the s(y + rf) − nk line is displaced upwards. The short-run equilibrium lies in point 1. In the medium run, the actual current account surplus per head goes beyond the required level, so foreign assets per head recover. In due course, the economy gravitates towards a new steady state. Foreign assets per head do no longer move. What is more, the terminal value surpasses the initial value. In the diagram, this is represented by point 2. The time pattern of foreign assets per head can be seen in figure 36.

Besides we examine consumption per head c = (1 − s)(rk + w + rf). In the short run, capital per head and the wage rate go up, whereas foreign assets per head come down. Properly speaking, the fall in foreign assets per head is equal in amount to the rise in capital per head $\Delta f = - \Delta k$. For this reason, consumption per head improves. And in the intermediate run, as foreign assets per head are piled up, consumption per head becomes even better. Figure 37 shows how consumption per head evolves.

At this juncture, we leave the one-time technical progress and turn to the international diffusion of technical knowledge, restricting ourselves to a rough outline. The basic idea is that an innovation in country 1 is followed by an imitation in country 2. Originally, let the world be in the steady state. The foreign positions are balanced. Against this background, an innovation takes place in country 1. Therefore capital moves from country 2 to country 1. Country 1 becomes a

57

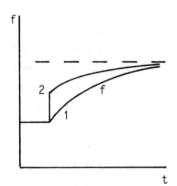

Figure 34
Foreign Assets Per Head

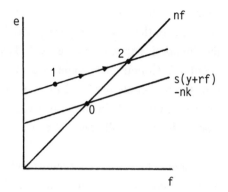

Figure 35
Technical Progress

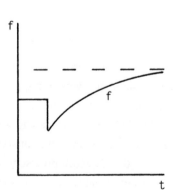

Figure 36
Foreign Assets Per Head

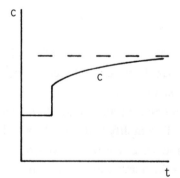

Figure 37
Consumption Per Head

debtor, and country 2 a creditor. In the medium run, foreign debt per head of country 1 diminishes. Simultaneously, foreign assets per head of country 2 are cut back. In the new steady state, the foreign positions are balanced again. Now the imitation happens in country 2. That is why capital moves from country 1 to country 2. Country 1 becomes a creditor, and country 2 a debtor. In the medium run, foreign assets per head of country 1 decline, and so does foreign debt per head of country 2. In the new steady state, the foreign positions are balanced again. This is the full debt cycle of innovation and imitation.

Coming to an end, continuous technical progress will be sketched out briefly. The relation $f/y = (s - \alpha n/r)/(n - rs)$ does still hold. The only difference is that here n includes both the rate of population growth and the rate of technical progress. As a result, the country characterized by fast technical progress will be a debtor. It experiences a current account deficit and a trade surplus. Conversely, the country characterized by slow technical progress will be a creditor. It registers a current account surplus and a trade deficit.

2. Overlapping Generations

In section 1, we considered a Solow model that was characterized by a fixed saving rate. In the current section, instead, we shall assume an overlapping generations model, featuring the intertemporal optimization of private agents within a finite horizon. Firms manufacture a single commodity by employing capital and labour. To simplify matters, take a Cobb-Douglas technology exhibiting constant returns to scale $Y = K^{\alpha} N^{\beta}$ with $\alpha > 0$, $\beta > 0$ and $\alpha + \beta = 1$. More precisely, N denotes the number of active workers. The labour market does always clear. Domestic output can be devoted to consumption, investment and net exports. Let labour grow at the natural rate $N_{+1} = (1+n)N$ with n = const. Here N symbolizes labour this period and N_{+1} labour next period.

For the small open economy, the foreign interest rate is given $r^* = $ const. Under perfect capital mobility, the domestic interest rate coincides with the foreign interest rate $r = r^*$. Firms maximize profits $\Pi = Y - rK - wN$ under perfect competition. Accordingly, the marginal product of capital is governed by the interest rate $\alpha Y/K = r$. On the other hand, the wage rate is determined by the marginal product of labour $w = \beta Y/N$.

Now have a look at dynamics, beginning with capital dynamics. In full analogy to section 1, $Y = K^\alpha N^\beta$, $r = \alpha Y/K$ and $N_{+1} = (1+n)N$ involve $K_{+1} = (1+n)K$.

We turn next to the centrepiece of dynamics, i.e. to the dynamics of foreign assets. The individual lifecycle is composed of two periods, the working period and the retirement period. During the working period, the individual receives labour income, which he partly consumes and partly saves. The savings are used to buy domestic bonds and foreign bonds. During the retirement period, the individual earns interest on the bonds and sells the bonds altogether. The proceeds are entirely consumed, no bequests are left.

The utility u of the representative individual depends on his consumption in the working period c^1 and on his consumption in the retirement period c^2. Take a logarithmic utility function $u = \gamma \log c^1 + \delta \log c^2$ with $\gamma > 0$, $\delta > 0$ and $\gamma + \delta = 1$. The budget constraint of the representative individual covers the whole lifecycle. w is labour income in the working period, and $w - c^1$ are savings in the working period. The individual earns the interest rate r on savings, so consumption in the retirement period is $c^2 = (w - c^1)(1+r)$. As a consequence, the individual budget constraint can be stated as $c^1 + c^2/(1+r) = w$. The individual chooses present and future consumption so as to maximize utility subject to his budget constraint. The evaluation of the Lagrange function yields consumption per head in the working period $c^1 = \gamma w$. Labour income minus consumption per head gives savings per head $s = w - c^1$ or $s = \delta w$. The savings of the active generation amount to $S = sN$. Observe $s = \delta w$ and $w = \beta Y/N$ to arrive at $S = \beta \delta Y$. The savings of the young generation serve to finance foreign assets and domestic capital of the subsequent period $F_{+1} + K_{+1} = S$. From this one can infer $F_{+1} + K_{+1} = \beta \delta Y$. Besides note $K_{+1} = (1+n)K$ and regroup $F_{+1} = \beta \delta Y - (1+n)K$.

60

On this foundation, the model can be represented by a system of four equations:

$$Y = K^{\alpha} N^{\beta} \tag{1}$$

$$r = \alpha Y / K \tag{2}$$

$$F_{+1} = \beta \delta Y - (1+n)K \tag{3}$$

$$N_{+1} = (1+n)N \tag{4}$$

Here α, β, δ, n, r, F and N are exogenous, while F_{+1}, K, N_{+1} and Y are endogenous.

It proves useful to do the analysis in per capita terms. (3) can be expressed as $(1+n)f_{+1} = \beta\delta y - (1+n)k$, where $f_{+1} = F_{+1} / N_{+1}$ stands for foreign assets per head (of the young), $y = Y/N$ is output per head, and $k = K/N$ is capital per head. Correspondingly, the model can be written down as a system of three equations:

$$y = k^{\alpha} \tag{5}$$

$$r = \alpha y / k \tag{6}$$

$$(1+n)f_{+1} = \beta \delta y - (1+n)k \tag{7}$$

Here α, β, δ, f, n and r are fixed, whereas f_{+1}, k and y are flexible.

From (5) and (6) one can deduce:

$$k = (\alpha / r)^{1/\beta} \tag{11}$$

$$y = (\alpha / r)^{\alpha/\beta} \tag{12}$$

As a finding, an increase in the foreign interest rate reduces both capital per head and output per head. An increase in δ, which can be viewed as a measure of patience, has no influence on capital per head and output per head whatsoever. The same applies to an increase in the rate of population growth. Essentially, this underlines the importance of the conclusions drawn in the Solow model.

In the steady state, the motion of foreign assets per head comes to a halt $f_{+1} = f$. Therefore the steady state can be described by:

$$y = k^{\alpha} \tag{8}$$

$$r = \alpha y / k \tag{9}$$

$$(1+n)f + (1+n)k = \beta \delta y \tag{10}$$

Here α, β, δ, n and r are given, while f, k and y adjust themselves.

Further we shall probe into stability. The model can be condensed to a first-order difference equation $f_{+1} = g(f)$. Get rid of y in (7) by means of (5) to reach:

$$f_{+1} = \frac{\beta \delta k^{\alpha}}{1+n} - k \tag{13}$$

Then differentiate (13) for f to realize:

$$\frac{df_{+1}}{df} = 0 \tag{14}$$

Judging by (14), the steady state is stable. This differs to a certain extent from the Solow model, where we derived a stability condition.

At this point, we shall address the basic characteristics of the steady state. Solve (10) for f:

$$f = \frac{\beta \delta y}{1+n} - k \tag{15}$$

Besides pay attention to (9):

$$\frac{f}{y} = \frac{\beta \delta}{1+n} - \frac{\alpha}{r} \tag{16}$$

This is the foreign asset ratio. (16) gives rise to two cases. If $\delta \gtrless \alpha(1+n)/\beta r$, then $f/y \gtrless 0$. That means, the high-saving country (i.e. the patient country) will be a creditor. The other way round, the low-saving country (i.e. the impatient country) will be a debtor.

What is more, an increase in patience causes an increase in the foreign asset ratio. Conversely, an increase in the rate of labour growth leads to a reduction in the foreign asset ratio. And an increase in the foreign interest rate produces an increase in the foreign asset ratio. This confirms the results obtained in the Solow model.

Correspondingly, figure 38 shows the foreign asset ratio as a function of patience. Likewise figure 39 illustrates the effect of the rate of labour growth on the foreign asset ratio. And figure 40 graphs how the foreign asset ratio varies as the foreign interest rate changes. Similarly figure 41 displays foreign assets per head as a function of the foreign interest rate. An increase in the foreign interest rate at first pushes up foreign assets per head, but later on pulls them down again. There are two critical levels of the foreign interest rate, $r' = \alpha(1 + n)/\beta\delta$ and $r'' = (1 + n)/\beta\delta$.

In addition regard the current account surplus ratio. Substitute (16) into $e = nf$ and rearrange:

$$\frac{e}{y} = \frac{\beta\delta n}{1+n} - \frac{\alpha n}{r} \tag{17}$$

Evidently a rise in patience brings up the current account surplus ratio. Starting from $e = 0$, a rise in the rate of population growth cuts back the current account surplus ratio. And a rise in the foreign interest rate boosts the current account surplus ratio. Figure 42 plots the current account surplus ratio as a function of the rate of population growth. All of these diagrams differ more or less from those in the Solow model, see above.

At last a few remarks will be made on the trade deficit ratio. Throw out f in $q = (r - n)f$ with the help of (16):

$$\frac{q}{y} = (r-n)\left[\frac{\beta\delta}{1+n} - \frac{\alpha}{r}\right] \tag{18}$$

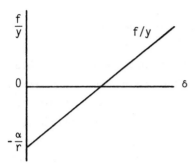

Figure 38
Saving Rate and
Foreign Asset Ratio

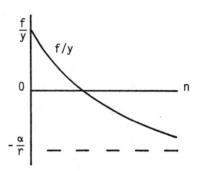

Figure 39
Growth Rate and
Foreign Asset Ratio

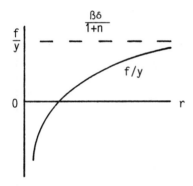

Figure 40
Foreign Interest Rate
and Foreign Asset Ratio

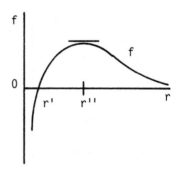

Figure 41
Foreign Interest Rate and
Foreign Assets Per Head

Let $r > n$. An increase in patience enhances the trade deficit ratio. An increase in the rate of labour growth, however, depresses the trade deficit ratio. And an increase in the foreign interest rate augments the trade deficit ratio.

In summary, an increase in patience leaves no impact on capital per head or output per head, but it raises the foreign asset ratio. An increase in the rate of population growth does affect neither capital per head nor output per head, yet it lowers the foreign asset ratio. An increase in the foreign interest rate reduces both capital per head and output per head. On the other hand, it raises the foreign asset ratio. In principle, this agrees with the findings in the Solow model. Table 9 offers a synopsis. The high-saving country (i.e. the patient country) will be a creditor. It runs a current account surplus and a trade deficit. An increase in patience drives up the foreign asset ratio, the current account surplus ratio and the trade deficit ratio.

Table 9
Long-Run Effects (Overlapping Generations)

	δ	n	r
k	0	0	–
y	0	0	–
f/y	+	–	+
e/y	+	–	+
q/y	+	–	+

Coming to an end, we shed some light on transitional dynamics. The equation of motion is given by (13) together with $k = (\alpha / r)^{1/\beta}$. First imagine a rise in patience. Therefore, with a one-period delay (i.e. a one-generation delay), foreign assets per head jump from the old steady state up to the new one. For the time path see figure 43. Second contemplate a rise in the rate of labour growth. The other way round, with a lag of one period, foreign assets per head jump from the old steady state down to the new one.

Third postulate a rise in the foreign interest rate. To make this clear, take a numerical example with $\alpha = 0.2$, $\beta = 0.8$, $\gamma = 0.7$ and $\delta = 0.3$. Let the working period and the retirement period each consist of 30 years. Let the rate of labour growth be $n = 1.427$ over a period of 30 years, which boils down to an annual rate of 3%. Beyond that, let the foreign interest rate be $r = 2.0225$ over a period of 30 years, which is equivalent to an annual rate of 3.8%. As an outcome, capital per head amounts to $k = (\alpha / r)^{1/\beta} = 0.05545$, output per head is $y = (\alpha / r)^{\alpha/\beta} = 0.5608$ and foreign assets per head are $f = \beta\delta y/(1 + n) - k = 0$. In these circumstances, the foreign interest rate goes up from 2.0225 to 3. Then, instantaneously, capital per head drops to 0.03388 and output per head skrinks to 0.5081. That is to say, capital per head diminishes by 0.02157. The rise in foreign assets per head equals the fall in capital per head, so foreign assets per head end up with $f = 0.02157$. Further, with a one-period delay, foreign assets per head decline to 0.01636. Figure 44 presents the associated time path.

3. Inifinite Horizon

The Solow model in section 1 was based on a fixed saving rate. The overlapping generations model in section 2 rested on intertemporal optimization within a finite horizon. Now the Ramsey model in the current section will be built on intertemporal optimization within an infinite horizon. The investigation will be carried out within the following setting. Firms produce a homogeneous commodity $Y = K^\alpha N^\beta$. The marginal product of capital harmonizes with the foreign interest rate $r = \alpha Y/K$. Domestic output goes to consumption, investment and net exports $Y = C + I + X$. Investment equals capital multiplied by the natural rate $I = nK$. The current account surplus is the sum of net exports and the interest

66

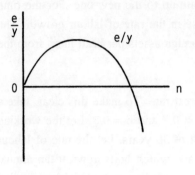

Figure 42
Current Account Surplus Ratio

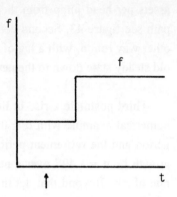

Figure 43
Increase in Saving Rate

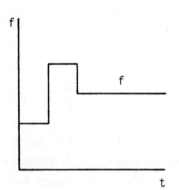

Figure 44
Increase in Foreign Interest Rate

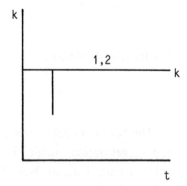

Figure 45
Capital Per Head

inflow $E = X + rF$. The current account surplus, on its part, contributes to the accumulation of foreign assets $\dot{F} = E$. Labour grows at the natural rate $\dot{N} = nN$. Let the foreign interest rate be greater than the natural rate $r > n$.

Eliminate X in $E = X + rF$ by making use of $Y = C + I + X$ to get $E = Y - C - I + rF$. Then insert this into $\dot{F} = E$, paying heed to $I = nK$, which yields $\dot{F} = Y - C - nK + rF$. It is convenient to perform the analysis in per capita terms. Take the time derivative of foreign assets per head $f = F/N$ to reach $\dot{f} = \dot{F}/N - F\dot{N}/N^2$. Then substitute $\dot{F} = Y - C - nK + rF$ to arrive at $\dot{f} = y + (r-n)f - c - nk$.

Having laid this groundwork, the model can be captured by a system of five equations:

$$y = k^{\alpha} \tag{1}$$

$$r = \alpha y / k \tag{2}$$

$$y = c + i + x \tag{3}$$

$$i = nk \tag{4}$$

$$\dot{f} = y + (r-n)f - c - nk \tag{5}$$

Here α, f, n and r are exogenous, while c, $\dot{f}$, i, k, x and y are endogenous. The number of variables exceeds the number of equations by one, so there still exists a degree of freedom.

Households maximize their utility within an infinite horizon:

$$W = \int_0^{\infty} \log(c)\exp(-\rho t)dt \to \max_c \tag{6}$$

subject to

$$\dot{f} = y + (r-n)f - c - nk \tag{7}$$

$\log(c)$ stands for the utility function, and ρ is the discount rate. Let $\rho = r - n$, otherwise there would be no steady state.

The solution to this problem is:

$$\dot{c} = \dot{f} = 0 \tag{8}$$

As a consequence, consumption per head and foreign assets per head are uniform. This together with (7) provides the level of consumption per head:

$$c = y + (r - n)f - nk \tag{9}$$

Here f denotes the initial value. For the method see e.g. Blanchard and Fischer (1989) as well as Chiang (1992). Of course, the model rests on rather strong assumptions. Above all, perfect foresight within an infinite horizon is taken for granted. Incidentally, the consumption function can be stated as $c = (1 - s)(y + rf)$. It goes without saying that here the saving rate is endogenous.

On this foundation, the model can be encapsulated in a system of six equations:

$$y = k^{\alpha} \tag{10}$$

$$r = \alpha y / k \tag{11}$$

$$c = y + (r - n)f - nk \tag{12}$$

$$i = nk \tag{13}$$

$$y = c + i + x \tag{14}$$

$$c = (1 - s)(y + rf) \tag{15}$$

In this instance, α, f, n and r are given, whereas c, i, k, s, x and y adjust themselves.

Put (12) and (13) into (14) to check $x = - (r - n)f$. This can be reformulated as:

$$q = (r - n)f \tag{16}$$

where q symbolizes net imports per head. Further extract s from (12) and (15):

$$s = \frac{nf + nk}{y + rf} \tag{17}$$

This is the optimal saving rate. What is more, the steady state is identical to the temporary equilibrium contained in (10) to (15).

For the remainder of this section, we shall deal with the process of adjustment. As a shock imagine a one-time increase in labour. Strictly speaking, this shock is superimposed on continuous labour growth at the constant rate n. At the beginning, the economy is in the steady state. Foreign assets per head and capital per head do not move. Against this background, labour increases, thereby reducing both foreign assets per head and capital per head. For that reason, instantaneously, capital flows in. This restores capital per head but reduces foreign assets per head once more. In this step, the fall in foreign assets per head is equivalent to the rise in capital per head $\Delta f = - \Delta k$. In the short-run equilibrium after shock, capital per head is back at its original level, while foreign assets per head lie well below their original level. With this, the process of adjustment is complete. In other words, the economy is in the new steady state. Foreign assets per head and capital per head do not move any longer.

Next transitional dynamics will be studied in greater detail. As a starting point, we have a one-time jump in foreign assets per head $\Delta f < 0$. First take the relevant differences of (12) to ascertain:

$$\Delta c = (r - n)\Delta f \tag{18}$$

Accordingly, the drop in foreign assets per head implies a drop in consumption per head. Thus there will be a one-time jump in consumption per head. Second take differences of (16) to find out:

$$\Delta q = (r - n)\Delta f \tag{19}$$

Likewise, the decline in foreign assets per head leads to a decline in net imports per head. Hence there will be a one-time jump in net imports per head, too. Third take differences of (15). As a good approximation one can obtain $\Delta c = r\Delta f - y\Delta s - r(f\Delta s - s\Delta f)$. Compare this with (18) to verify:

$$\Delta s = \frac{n - rs}{y + rf} \Delta f \tag{20}$$

Let $n > rs$. Then the cut in foreign assets per head brings about a cut in the saving rate. So there will be a one-time jump in the saving rate as well.

In summary, there will be a one-time jump in foreign assets per head, consumption per head, net imports per head and the saving rate. For the time paths see figures 45 until 49. Time path number 1, respectively, is generated by the Ramsey model. Time path number 2, as a point of reference, is generated by the Solow model.

To illustrate this, consider a numerical example with $\alpha = 0.2$, $n = 0.03$, $r = 0.06$ and initial value $f_0 = 0$. Let us begin with the steady state before shock. Capital per head totals $k = (\alpha / r)^{1/\beta} = 4.5040$, output per head is $y = k^{\alpha} = 1.3512$, consumption per head is $c = y + (r - n)f - nk = 1.2161$, and investment per head is $i = nk = 0.1351$. Due to $y = c + i + x$, net exports are $x = 0$. Owing to $c = (1 - s)(y + rf)$, the saving rate is $s = 0.1000$.

In this situation, labour increases by 10%. On this ground, capital per head diminishes from 4.5040 to 4.0945. Here foreign assets per head do not respond f = 0, for the sole reason that they were zero at the start. Therefore, at once, capital flows in. Capital per head rises from 4.0945 to 4.5040, so foreign assets per head fall from 0 to $- 0.4095$. In the short-run equilibrium after shock, capital per head and output head have come back to their original level $k = 4.5040$ and $y = 1.3512$. Foreign assets per head are $f = - 0.4095$. Consumption per head is lower $c = 1.2038$, investment per head is the same $i = 0.1351$, net exports per head are higher $x = 0.0123$, and the saving rate is lower $s = 0.0926$. Beyond that, the steady state after shock is identical to the short-run equilibrium after shock. Table 10 presents an overview of the process. To conclude, a 10% increase in labour causes a 1% reduction in consumption per head and a 7% reduction in the saving rate.

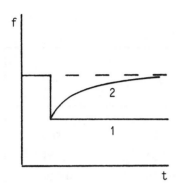

Figure 46
Foreign Assets Per Head

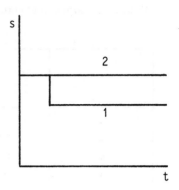

Figure 47
Optimal Saving Rate

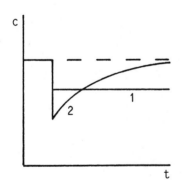

Figure 48
Consumption Per Head

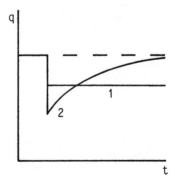

Figure 49
Trade Deficit Per Head

Table 10
Process of Adjustment (Infinite Horizon)

	0	1	∞
k	4.504	4.504	4.504
y	1.351	1.351	1.351
f	0	− 0.410	− 0.410
c	1.216	1.204	1.204
i	0.135	0.135	0.135
x	0	0.012	0.012
s	0.100	0.093	0.093

CHAPTER II. TWO COUNTRIES

1. Different Saving Rates (Overlapping Generations)

1.1. Steady State

In the current chapter, we change from the small open economy to a world being composed of two large countries. Buiter (1981) did a very careful and thorough analysis of two countries inhabited by overlapping generations. Therefore we shall confine ourselves to a rather short presentation. Along the same lines as in the preceding chapter, the model consists of nine equations:

$$Y_i = K_i^\alpha N_i^\beta \tag{1}$$

$$r = \alpha Y_i / K_i \tag{2}$$

$$F_i^{+1} + K_i^{+1} = \beta \delta_i Y_i \tag{3}$$

$$N_i^{+1} = (1+n) N_i \tag{4}$$

$$F_1 = -F_2 \tag{5}$$

The index $i = 1, 2$ denotes the country in question. In equation (1), identical technologies are assumed across countries. Equation (2) states that the interest rate matches the marginal product of capital. Under perfect capital mobility, the interest rates are the same in both countries $r = r_1 = r_2$. Here the interest rate is endogenous, contrary to the small open economy. By virtue of equation (3), the savings of the young this period give foreign assets and domestic capital next period. Let the countries differ in patience $\delta_1 \neq \delta_2$. Equation (4) is based on the premise that labour grows at the uniform rate $n = n_1 = n_2$ worldwide. Equation (5) has it that the foreign assets of country 1 coincide with the foreign debt of country 2. Here α, β, δ_i, n, F_i, K_i and N_i are exogenous, while r, F_i^{+1}, K_i^{+1}, N_i^{+1} and Y_i are endogenous. Thus the number of equations agrees with the number of variables.

At this point we switch to per capita terms. $f_i^{+1} = F_i^{+1}/N_i^{+1}$ symbolizes foreign assets per head, and $k_i^{+1} = K_i^{+1}/N_i^{+1}$ is capital per head. With these definitions,

(3) can be transformed into $(1 + n)f_i^{+1} + (1 + n)k_i^{+1} = \beta\delta_i y_i$. Let population be the same size in both countries $N_1 = N_2$, hence (5) turns into $f_1 = - f_2$. Assembling all component parts, the model can be described by a system of seven equations:

$$y_i = k_i^\alpha \tag{6}$$

$$r = \alpha y_i / k_i \tag{7}$$

$$(1+n)f_i^{+1} + (1+n)k_i^{+1} = \beta\delta_i y_i \tag{8}$$

$$f_1 = -f_2 \tag{9}$$

Here α, β, δ_i, f_i, k_i and n are fixed, whereas f_i^{+1}, k_i^{+1}, r and y_i are flexible.

In the steady state, foreign assets per head and capital per head come to a halt $f_i^{+1} = f_i$ and $k_i^{+1} = k_i$. Correspondingly, the steady state can be written down as a system of seven equations:

$$y_i = k_i^\alpha \tag{10}$$

$$r = \alpha y_i / k_i \tag{11}$$

$$(1+n)f_i + (1+n)k_i = \beta\delta_i y_i \tag{12}$$

$$f_1 = -f_2 \tag{13}$$

At this stage, α, β, δ_i and n are given, while f_i, k_i, r and y_i adjust themselves.

What about the distinguishing qualities of the steady state? Compare (10) and (11) to attain $k_1 = k_2$ and $y_1 = y_2$. That is to say, the countries are identical in both capital per head and output per head. Then take the sum of (12), noting $f_1 = - f_2$, $k_1 = k_2$ and $y_1 = y_2$ to get $2(1 + n)k_1 = (\delta_1 + \delta_2)\beta y_1$. Further throw out y_1 with the help of $y_1 = k_1^\alpha$ and reshuffle terms to conclude:

$$k_1^\beta = \frac{\beta(\delta_1 + \delta_2)}{2(1+n)} \tag{14}$$

An increase in the saving rate (i.e. the patience) of country 1 raises capital per head in each of the countries. On account of symmetry, the same applies to an increase in the saving rate of country 2. And an increase in the rate of labour growth lowers capital per head in both countries.

The next point refers to the foreign assets held by country 1. Eliminate k_1 in $(1+n)f_1 + (1+n)k_1 = \beta\delta_1 y_1$ by means of (14) to arrive at:

$$f_1 = \frac{(\delta_1 - \delta_2)\beta y_1}{2(1+n)} \qquad (15)$$

Moreover substitute $y_1 = k_1^\alpha$ into (15), observing again (14), to reach:

$$f_1^\beta = (\delta_1 + \delta_2)^\alpha (\delta_1 - \delta_2)^\beta \frac{\beta}{2(1+n)} \qquad (16)$$

The evaluation of (15) and (16), respectively, gives rise to two cases. If $\delta_1 > \delta_2$, then country 1 will be a creditor, and country 2 a debtor. On the other hand, if $\delta_1 < \delta_2$, then country 1 will be a debtor, and country 2 a creditor. Put another way, the high-saving country (i.e. the patient country) will be a creditor. Conversely, the low-saving country (i.e. the impatient country) will be a debtor.

Now let the saving rate of country 1 be greater than the saving rate of country 2, so country 1 will be a creditor, and country 2 a debtor. Then an increase in the saving rate of country 1 augments both foreign assets per head of country 1 and foreign debt per head of country 2. The other way round, an increase in the saving rate of country 2 diminishes both foreign assets per head of country 1 and foreign debt per head of country 2. What is more, country 1 may change from a creditor to a debtor position. In this instance, country 2 would become a creditor. Now let the saving rate of country 1 still surpass the saving rate of country 2, hence country 1 continues to be a creditor, and country 2 a debtor. Then an increase in the rate of population growth reduces both foreign assets per head of country 1 and foreign debt per head of country 2.

In addition, the current account surplus per head of country 1 amounts to $e_1 = nf_1$, and the trade deficit per head of country 1 is $q_1 = (r - n)f_1$. We posit $r > n$. Once more, let the saving rate of country 1 exceed the saving rate of country 2. In this situation, country 1 runs a current account surplus, and country 2 a current account deficit, where the surplus of country 1 equals the deficit of country

2. Similarly country 1 incurs a trade deficit, and country 2 a trade surplus, such that the deficit of country 1 is the same size as the surplus of country 2.

Over and above that, an increase in the saving rate of country 1 brings up both the current account surplus per head of country 1 and the current account deficit per head of country 2. Likewise, the shock enhances both the trade deficit per head of country 1 and the trade surplus per head of country 2. However, an increase in the saving rate of country 2 cuts back both the current account surplus per head of country 1 and the current account deficit per head of country 2. In analogy, it depresses the trade deficit per head of country 1 and the trade surplus per head of country 2. If the shock is sufficiently large, the current account surplus of country 1 turns into a deficit, and the trade deficit of country 1 turns into a surplus. That means, the current account deficit of country 2 is transformed into a surplus, and the trade surplus of country 2 is transformed into a deficit. Last but not least, figure 1 shows the current account surplus per head of country 1 as a function of the rate of labour growth, on the condition that $\delta_1 > \delta_2$. At first the current account surplus per head goes up, yet later on it comes down again.

In summary, the high-saving country will be a creditor. It experiences a current account surplus and a trade deficit. The low-saving country, on the other hand, will be a debtor. It registers a current account deficit and a trade surplus. Now let country 1 be a creditor, and country 2 a debtor. Then an increase in the saving rate of country 1 raises capital per head in each of the countries. Moreover the shock drives up both foreign assets per head of country 1 and foreign debt per head of country 2. The interest rate falls worldwide, whereas the wage rate rises. This is in remarkable contrast to the results obtained for the small open economy. Table 11 offers a synopsis.

Finally, what are the main differences between the small open economy and the two-country world? The small open economy can be characterized as follows. First, the high-saving country will be a creditor. Second, the fast-growing country will be a debtor. And third, when the foreign interest rate is high, the country in question will be a creditor. As opposed to that, the two-country world can be characterized by a single sentence: The high-saving country will be a creditor. The second and the third point cannot be made here. The reasons for this are that the countries expand at the same rate, and that the interest rate is endogenous.

Table 11
Long-Run Effects (Two Countries)

	δ_1	δ_2	n
k_1	+	+	−
k_2	+	+	−
f_1	+	−	−
d_2	+	−	−
r	−	−	+
w	+	+	−

1.2. Process of Adjustment

To begin with, we shall inquire into stability. The model can be compressed to a system of two difference equations:

$$f_1^{+1} = g(f_1, k_1) \tag{17}$$
$$k_1^{+1} = h(f_1, k_1) \tag{18}$$

At first take the sum of (8), paying attention to $f_1 = -f_2$, $k_1 = k_2$ and $y_1 = y_2$, which yields $2(1+n)k_1^{+1} = (\delta_1 + \delta_2)\beta y_1$. Now insert $y_1 = k_1^{\alpha}$ and regroup:

78

$$k_1^{+1} = \frac{(\delta_1 + \delta_2)\beta k_1^\alpha}{2(1+n)} \tag{19}$$

Then differentiate (19) for k_1 and evaluate at the steady state with (14) to realize:

$$\frac{\partial k_1^{+1}}{\partial k_1} = \alpha < 1 \tag{20}$$

Further set $k_1^{+1} = k_1$ in (19) and solve for k_1^β:

$$k_1^\beta = \frac{\beta(\delta_1 + \delta_2)}{2(1+n)} \tag{21}$$

As a finding, k_1 does not depend on f_1. Accordingly figure 2 depicts the horizontal kk demarcation line.

Moreover get rid of k_1^{+1} in (8) by making use of $2(1+n)k_1^{+1} = (\delta_1 + \delta_2)\beta y_1$ to ascertain $2(1+n)f_1^{+1} = (\delta_1 - \delta_2)\beta y_1$. In addition substitute $y_1 = k_1^\alpha$, which provides:

$$f_1^{+1} = \frac{(\delta_1 - \delta_2)\beta k_1^\alpha}{2(1+n)} \tag{22}$$

Consider the case $\delta_1 > \delta_2$. Then f_1^{+1} rises as k_1 rises. Besides put $f_1^{+1} = f_1$ into (22) to check:

$$f_1 = \frac{(\delta_1 - \delta_2)\beta k_1^\alpha}{2(1+n)} \tag{23}$$

Once more let $\delta_1 > \delta_2$, so a lift in k_1 causes a lift in f_1. Figure 2 portrays the upward sloping ff demarcation line. The steady state proves to be stable, as can be learnt from the phase diagram.

At this juncture, we leave stability and turn to the process of adjustment proper. More precisely, we shall discuss the dynamic consequences of an increase in the saving rate of country 1, assuming $\delta_1 > \delta_2$. Initially the world is at

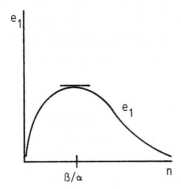

Figure 1
Growth Rate and
Current Account Surplus Per Head

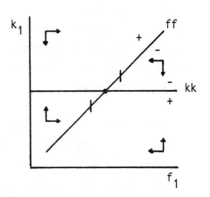

Figure 2
Two Countries (Country 1)

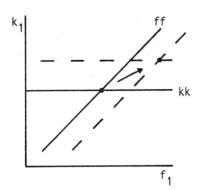

Figure 3
Increase in Saving Rate
of Country 1

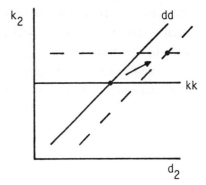

Figure 4
Increase in Saving Rate
of Country 1

80

rest in the steady state. In country 1, the current account surplus per head and foreign assets per head are constant. In country 2, equivalently, the current account
deficit per head and foreign debt per head do not vary. In both countries, investment per head and capital per head are uniform. Figure 3 represents country 1,
and figure 4 country 2. The steady state lies in the point of intersection between
the ff line and the kk line.

Then, abruptly, the saving rate of country 1 rises. In figure 3, therefore, the ff
line shifts to the right, whereas the kk line shifts upwards. In figure 4, correspondingly, the dd line travels to the right, while the kk line is displaced upwards.
In the short run, in country 1, the current account surplus per head and investment per head go up. Similarly, in country 2, the current account deficit per head
and investment per head are boosted. In the medium run, in country 1, this contributes to the accumulation of both foreign assets per head and capital per head.
In country 2, analogously, both foreign debt per head and capital per head start
growing. In figures 3 and 4, the streamlines indicate the ways in which the countries evolve.

Ultimately the world tends to a new steady state. In country 1, the current account surplus per head and foreign assets per head come to a standstill. In country 2, equivalently, the current account deficit per head and foreign debt per head
stop adjusting. In both countries, investment per head and capital per head do not
move any longer. Taking the sum over the process as a whole, foreign assets per
head of country 1, foreign debt per head of country 2, and capital per head in
each of the countries end up well above their original levels. Figures 5 till 7
visualize the accompanying time patterns. All of these figures are distinct from
those derived for the small open economy, see above.

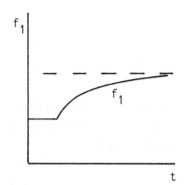

Figure 5
Foreign Assets Per Head
of Country 1

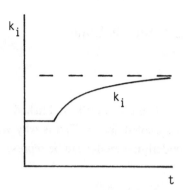

Figure 6
Capital Per Head

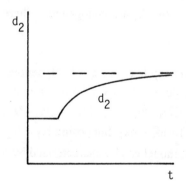

Figure 7
Foreign Debt Per Head
of Country 2

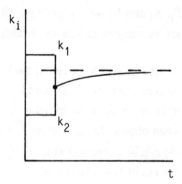

Figure 8
Capital Per Head

2. Different Saving Rates (Solow Model)

2.1. Steady State

There is a well-established body of literature on this subject, see the references quoted above. That is why we shall restrict ourselves to a rough outline. The underlying model can be represented by a system of nine equations:

$$Y_i = K_i^{\alpha} N_i^{\beta} \tag{1}$$

$$r = \alpha Y_i / K_i \tag{2}$$

$$\dot{F}_i + \dot{K}_i = s_i (Y_i + rF_i) \tag{3}$$

$$\dot{N}_i = nN_i \tag{4}$$

$$F_1 = -F_2 \tag{5}$$

In equation (1), we postulate identical technologies. Equation (2) is based on perfect capital mobility. Equation (3) has it that savings add to foreign assets and domestic capital. Let the countries differ in saving rates $s_1 \neq s_2$. Equation (4) states that population grows at the same uniform rate $n = n_1 = n_2$. Here α, n, s_i, F_i, K_i and N_i are exogenous, while r, $\dot{F}_i$, $\dot{K}_i$, $\dot{N}_i$ and Y_i are endogenous. There are as many equations as variables.

It is useful to carry out the investigation in per capita terms. $f_i = F_i/N_i$ denotes foreign assets per head, and $k_i = K_i/N_i$ is capital per head. Now take the time derivative of $f_i + k_i$ to gain $\dot{f}_i + \dot{k}_i = \dot{F}_i / N_i - F_i \dot{N}_i / N_i^2 + \dot{K}_i / N_i - K_i \dot{N}_i / N_i^2$. Then observe (3) to achieve $\dot{f}_i + \dot{k}_i = s_i (y_i + rf_i) - nf_i - nk_i$. Supposing $N_1 = N_2$, (5) can be expressed as $f_1 = -f_2$. In this way, the model can be characterized by a system of seven equations:

$$y_i = k_i^{\alpha} \tag{6}$$

$$r = \alpha y_i / k_i \tag{7}$$

$$\dot{f}_i + \dot{k}_i = s_i (y_i + rf_i) - nf_i - nk_i \tag{8}$$

$$f_1 = -f_2 \tag{9}$$

Here α, f_i, k_i, n and s_i are given, whereas $\dot{f}_i$, $\dot{k}_i$, r and y_i adjust themselves.

In the steady state, foreign assets per head and capital per head do no longer move $\dot{f}_i = \dot{k}_i = 0$. Accordingly the steady state can be caught by a system of seven equations:

$$y_i = k_i^{\alpha} \tag{10}$$

$$r = \alpha y_i / k_i \tag{11}$$

$$nf_i + nk_i = s_i(y_i + rf_i) \tag{12}$$

$$f_1 = -f_2 \tag{13}$$

Here α, n and s_i are fixed, while f_i, k_i, r and y_i are flexible.

What are the salient features of the steady state? From (10) and (11) one can deduce $k_1 = k_2$ and $y_1 = y_2$. Next take the sum of (12), noting $f_1 = -f_2$, $k_1 = k_2$ and $y_1 = y_2$, to find $2nk_1 = (s_1 + s_2)y_1 + (s_1 - s_2)rf_1$. Further dispense with r, paying heed to $r = \alpha y_1 / k_1$ and $v = k_1 / y_1$, where v symbolizes the capital-output ratio:

$$2nv = s_1 + s_2 + (s_1 - s_2)\frac{\alpha}{v}\frac{f_1}{y_1} \tag{14}$$

Besides substitute $r = \alpha y_1 / k_1$ as well as $v = k_1 / y_1$ into $nf_1 + nk_1 = s_1(y_1 + rf_1)$ and solve for the foreign asset ratio of country 1:

$$\frac{f_1}{y_1} = \frac{s_1 - nv}{n - \alpha s_1 / v} \tag{15}$$

Moreover combine (14) and (15) to arrive at:

$$2n^2v^2 - (1+\alpha)(s_1 + s_2)nv + 2\alpha s_1 s_2 = 0 \tag{16}$$

Evidently this is a quadratic equation in nv, yielding the capital-output ratio. Because of symmetry, the foreign asset ratio of country 2 is:

$$\frac{f_2}{y_2} = \frac{s_2 - nv}{n - \alpha s_2 / v} \tag{17}$$

As an upshot, three cases can occur. First, if $s_1 = s_2$, then $f_1 = f_2 = 0$. Second, if $s_1 > s_2$, then, $f_1 > 0$ and $f_2 < 0$. Third, if $s_1 < s_2$, then $f_1 < 0$ and $f_2 > 0$. In other words, the high-saving country will be a creditor. Conversely, the low-saving country will be a debtor.

To elucidate this, regard a numerical example with $\alpha = 0.2$, $n = 0.03$ and $s_2 = 0.1$. Correspondingly, table 12 displays the capital-output ratio and the foreign asset ratio of country 1, given the saving rate of country 1. Let us start with $s_1 = 0.1$. This implies $s_1 = s_2$, $v = 3.33$ and $f_1/y_1 = d_2/y_2 = 0$. That is to say, the foreign positions are balanced. Now imagine that the saving rate of country 1 goes up to $s_1 = 0.11$. From this follows $v = 3.50$ and $f_1/y_1 = d_2/y_2 = 0.21$. So foreign assets of country 1 are 21% of its output, and foreign debt of country 2 is 21% of its output, respectively. Compare this to the small open economy, where we found $f/y = 0.43$, which is about twice as much. Put another way, f/y roughly equals $f_1/y_1 + d_2/y_2$. In addition, there exists a second steady state with $v = 0.69802$ and $f_1/y_1 = -58.68$. Unfortunately, the second steady state turns out to be unstable. Instead imagine that the saving rate of country 1 comes down to $s_1 = 0.09$. This produces $v = 3.17$ and $d_1/y_1 = f_2/y_2 = 0.21$. Hence country 1 will be a borrower, and country 2 a lender.

In summary, an increase in the saving rate of country 1 pushes up the capital-output ratio. What is more, it drives up the foreign asset ratio of country 1. Clearly this differs from the conclusions drawn for the small open economy, where the capital-output ratio was invariant.

Table 12
Long-Run Effects (Two-Countries)

s_1	v	f_1/y_1
0	2	−2
0.05	2.5672	−1.0349
0.09	3.1689	−0.2083
0.10	3.3333	0
0.11	3.5020	0.2083
0.15	4.2078	1.0393
0.20	5.1344	2.0698

2.2. Introducing Capital Mobility

In this section, we shall proceed by making four steps. First, we shall determine the steady state without capital mobility. Second, we shall try to find out the short-run equilibrium with capital mobility. Third, we shall establish the steady state with capital mobility. And fourth, we shall present the resulting time paths.

Initially let the economy be in the steady state without capital mobility. This steady state can be captured by a system of four equations:

$$y_i = k_i^{\alpha} \tag{1}$$
$$nk_i = s_i y_i \tag{2}$$

Here α, n and s_i are exogenous, while k_i and y_i are endogenous. From (1) and (2) one can infer:

$$k_i = (s_i / n)^{1/\beta} \tag{3}$$
$$y_i = (s_i / n)^{\alpha/\beta} \tag{4}$$

World capital per head totals $k = (k_1 + k_2)/2$, and world output per head is $y = (y_1 + y_2)/2$. The interest rate is given by $r_i = \alpha y_i / k_i$, and consumption per head is $c_i = (1 - s_i) y_i$. To illuminate this, have a look at a numerical example with $\alpha = 0.2$, $n = 0.03$, $s_1 = 0.14$ and $s_2 = 0.06$. For the outcome see table 13, period 0.

At this point, we leave the steady state without capital mobility and turn to the short-run equilibrium with capital mobility. In the steady state without capital mobility, let the interest rate of country 1 fall short of the interest rate of country 2. Therefore, upon introducing capital mobility, capital moves instantaneously from country 1 to country 2. This reduces capital per head of country 1 and increases capital per head of country 2, until capital per head is equalized. Correspondingly, the interest rate of country 1 rises, whereas the interest rate of country 2 falls, until they are the same. In this process, the foreign assets per head of country 1 go up, while the foreign assets per head of country 2 come down. Properly speaking, the variation in foreign assets per head is equal in amount to the variation in capital per head $\Delta f_i = -\Delta k_i$.

In the numerical example, capital per head of country 1 drops from 6.86 to 4.62, that is by 67%. The other way round, capital per head of country 2 shoots up from 2.38 to 4.62, that is by 94%. World capital per head, however, remains fixed at 4.62. Likewise, output per head of country 1 is cut back from 1.47 to 1.36. Conversely, output per head of country 2 is boosted from 1.19 to 1.36. World output per head improves from 1.33 to 1.36, in spite of the fact that world capital per head does not change. This effect is due to the international reallocation of capital. The interest rate of country 1 mounts from 0.043 to 0.059, and the interest rate of country 2 descends from 0.100 to 0.059. The foreign assets per head of country 1 are raised from 0 to 2.24, so country 1 becomes a creditor. On the other hand, the foreign assets per head of country 2 are lowered from 0 to − 2.24, hence country 2 becomes a debtor. Consumption per head of country 1 expands from 1.264 to 1.281, that is by 1.3%. Similarly, consumption per head of country 2 grows from 1.118 to 1.153, that is by 3.1%. The differential effect can be ascribed to diminishing returns to substitution. For an overview see table 13, especially period 1.

Table 13
Process of Adjustment (Introducing Capital Mobility)

	0	1	∞
k_1	6.859	4.619	4.720
k_2	2.378	4.619	4.720
k	4.619	4.619	4.720
y_1	1.470	1.358	1.364
y_2	1.189	1.358	1.364
y	1.330	1.358	1.364
r_1	0.043	0.059	0.058
r_2	0.100	0.059	0.058
f_1	0	2.240	2.252
f_2	0	- 2.240	- 2.252
c_1	1.264	1.281	1.285
c_2	1.118	1.153	1.160

Next we throw some light on the medium-run implications. In the short run, capital mobility had brought up world income per head and thus world savings per head. In the intermediate run, for that reason, world capital per head accumulates period by period. Owing to that, world income per head and world consumption per head are pushed up even further. Asymptotically the economy converges to the steady state with capital mobility. Capital per head increases from 4.62 to 4.72, as compared to period 1. The interest rate declines from 0.059 to 0.058. The foreign assets per head of country 1 are lifted from 2.24 to 2.25. The

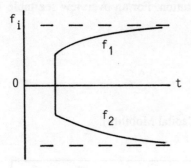

Figure 9
Foreign Assets Per Head

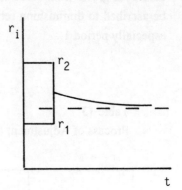

Figure 10
Interest Rates

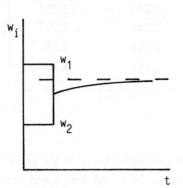

Figure 11
Wage Rates

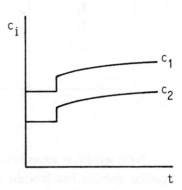

Figure 12
Consumption Per Head

same holds of the foreign debt per head of country 2. Consumption per head of country 1 continues to expand from 1.281 to 1.285, that is by 0.3%. And consumption per head of country 2 keeps on growing from 1.153 to 1.160, that is by 0.6%. The reader may wish to consult table 13, period ∞. Over the process of adjustment as a whole, capital mobility raises consumption per head in country 1 by 1.7%, in country 2 by 3.8% and at world level by 2.8%. Figures 8 till 12 graph how the countries travel through time.

In summary, capital mobility improves consumption per head in each of the countries at all times. But there is some redistribution involved. In the high-saving country, the interest rate goes up, whereas the wage rate comes down. Yet in the low-saving country, the interest rate is cut back, while the wage rate is bid up. If wages are not sufficiently flexible, then the high-saving country will suffer from unemployment.

3. Technical Progress Abroad (Solow Model)

3.1. Steady State

The reform countries in Central Eastern Europe and the newly industrialized countries in South East Asia are going to enter the world market. How will the advanced countries be affected by this? For instance, what will be the effects on capital flows and consumption? In the current section, we shall develop a two-country model, where country 1 represents the group of the advanced countries, and country 2 among others the group of the emerging countries. The shock that has just been mentioned can be interpreted, within the framework of this model, as a one-time technical progress abroad (i.e. in country 2).

The model consists of nine equations:

$$Y_i = \varepsilon_i K_i^\alpha N_i^\beta \tag{1}$$

$$r = \alpha Y_i / K_i \qquad (2)$$

$$\dot{F}_i + \dot{K}_i = s(Y_i + rF_i) \qquad (3)$$

$$\dot{N}_i = nN_i \qquad (4)$$

$$F_1 = -F_2 \qquad (5)$$

Equation (1) starts from the premise that the countries differ in technology $\varepsilon_1 \neq \varepsilon_2$, where ε_i denotes efficiency. Equation (3) rests on the assumption that saving rates are the same across countries $s = s_1 = s_2$, as opposed to the preceding sections. Here α, β, ε_i, n, s, F_i, K_i and N_i are exogenous, while r, $\dot{F}_i$, $\dot{K}_i$, $\dot{N}_i$ and Y_i are endogenous.

In per capita terms, the model is made up of seven equations:

$$y_i = \varepsilon_i k_i^{\alpha} \qquad (6)$$

$$r = \alpha y_i / k_i \qquad (7)$$

$$\dot{f}_i + \dot{k}_i = s(y_i + rf_i) - nf_i - nk_i \qquad (8)$$

$$f_1 = -f_2 \qquad (9)$$

Equation (9) presupposes equal populations $N_1 = N_2$. Here α, β, ε_i, f_i, k_i, n and s are given, whereas $\dot{f}_i$, $\dot{k}_i$, r and y_i adjust themselves.

In the steady state, foreign assets per head and capital per head do not move any more. Thus the steady state can be written down as follows:

$$y_i = \varepsilon_i k_i^{\alpha} \qquad (10)$$

$$r = \alpha y_i / k_i \qquad (11)$$

$$nf_i + nk_i = s(y_i + rf_i) \qquad (12)$$

$$f_1 = -f_2 \qquad (13)$$

Here α, β, ε_i, n and s are fixed, while f_i, k_i, r and y_i are variable.

We come now to the attributes of the steady state. Without losing generality, set $\varepsilon_i = 1$. Then combine (10) and (11):

$$\frac{y_2}{y_1} = \frac{k_2}{k_1} = \varepsilon_2^{1/\beta} \tag{14}$$

As a finding, an increase in the efficiency of country 2 raises both k_2/k_1 and y_2/y_1. In addition, take the sum of (12) and observe $f_1 = -f_2$ to get $nk_1 + nk_2 = sy_1 + sy_2$. Further eliminate k_2 and y_2 with the help of (14) to realize $nk_1 = sy_1$ and $nk_2 = sy_2$.

On these grounds, the steady state of country 1 can be encapsulated in a system of two equations:

$$y_1 = k_1^\alpha \tag{15}$$

$$nk_1 = sy_1 \tag{16}$$

From this one can conclude:

$$k_1 = (s/n)^{1/\beta} \tag{17}$$

$$y_1 = (s/n)^{\alpha/\beta} \tag{18}$$

As a consequence, an increase in the efficiency of country 2 leaves no impact on capital per head and output per head of country 1.

Similarly, the steady state of country 2 can be described by a system of two equations:

$$y_2 = \varepsilon_2 k_2^\alpha \tag{19}$$

$$nk_2 = sy_2 \tag{20}$$

This produces:

$$k_2 = (\varepsilon_2 s/n)^{1/\beta} \tag{21}$$

$$y_2 = \varepsilon_2 (\varepsilon_2 s/n)^{\alpha/\beta} \tag{22}$$

Judging by (21) and (22), an increase in the efficiency of country 2 brings up both capital per head and output per head of country 2.

Moreover confront $nf_1 + nk_1 = s(y_1 + rf_1)$ and $nk_1 = sy_1$ to check:

$$f_1 = 0 \tag{23}$$

As a result, the foreign positions are balanced. Of course this can be traced back to the assumption $s_1 = s_2$. Besides, an increase in the efficiency of country 2 does not impinge on the foreign positions. Consumption per head of country 1 amounts to $c_1 = (1-s)(y_1 + rf_1)$. Thanks to $f_1 = 0$, this simplifies to:

$$c_1 = (1-s)y_1 \tag{24}$$

In the same way one can derive:

$$c_2 = (1-s)y_2 \tag{25}$$

Therefore, an increase in the efficiency of country 2 does not influence consumption per head of country 1, but lifts that of country 2.

In summary, an increase in the efficiency of country 2 has no effect on capital per head and output per head of country 1. On the other hand, it raises capital per head and output per head of country 2. The foreign positions are always balanced. Consumption per head of country 1 does not respond, whereas that of country 2 improves.

What about stability? The model can be condensed to a system of two differential equations:

$$\dot{f}_1 = g(f_1, k_1) \tag{26}$$
$$\dot{k}_1 = h(f_1, k_1) \tag{27}$$

At first take the sum of (8), noting $f_1 = -f_2$, which yields $\dot{k}_1 + \dot{k}_2 = s(y_1 + y_2) - n(k_1 + k_2)$. Now get rid of y_2, k_2 and $\dot{k}_2$ by means of (14):

$$\dot{k}_1 = sy_1 - nk_1 \tag{28}$$

Then put this into (8):

$$\dot{f}_1 = srf_1 - nf_1 \tag{29}$$

Further dispense with y_1 in (28), drawing on (7):

$$\dot{k}_1 = sk_1^\alpha - nk_1 \tag{30}$$

Then differentiate this for k_1 and evaluate the ensuing term at the steady state with (17):

$$\frac{\partial \dot{k}_1}{\partial k_1} = -\beta n < 0 \tag{31}$$

Moreover set $\dot{k}_1 = 0$ to accomplish:

$$k_1 = (s/n)^{1/\beta} \tag{32}$$

Figure 13 depicts the horizontal $\dot{k}_1 = 0$ demarcation line.

Beyond that try to do without r in (29) by having recourse to $r = \alpha k_1^{-\beta}$:

$$\dot{f}_1 = \alpha sf_1 k_1^{-\beta} - nf_1 \tag{33}$$

Likewise differentiate (33) for f_1 and evaluate at the steady state with (17):

$$\frac{\partial \dot{f}_1}{\partial f_1} = -\beta n < 0 \tag{34}$$

Finally set $\dot{f}_1 = 0$ to arrive at:

$$f_1 = 0 \tag{35}$$

Figure 13 plots the vertical $\dot{f}_1 = 0$ demarcation line. The message conveyed by the phase diagram is that the steady state will be stable. In full analogy, figure 14 contains the phase diagram of country 2.

3.2. Process of Adjustment

Here we shall look into the transitional dynamics of a one-time technical progress abroad. At the beginning the economy is in the long-run equilibrium. In each of the countries, let the current account and the foreign position be balanced. In both countries, investment per head and capital per head are uniform. The interest rates and the marginal products of capital are equalized among countries. In the phase diagram, the permanent equilibrium is situated at the crossroads of the $\dot{f}_i = 0$ and $\dot{k}_i = 0$ lines, cf. figures 13 and 14.

Against this background, efficiency rises in country 2. This drives up the marginal product of capital in country 2, thereby raising its interest rate. Instantaneously, because of this, capital flows from country 1 to country 2. Capital per head of country 1 comes down, while capital per head of country 2 goes up. That is why the marginal product of capital in country 1 augments, whereas the marginal product of capital in country 2 diminishes. This process stops only when the marginal products of capital are once more the same. In country 1, a large current account surplus occurs that gives rise to foreign assets. And in country 2, owing to the large current account deficit, foreign debt enters the scene. In the phase diagrams, the $\dot{k}_2 = 0$ line shifts upwards. Besides the shock depresses k_1 and enhances k_2. In addition, we have $f_1 > 0$ and $f_2 < 0$, see figures 13 and 14.

We tackle next the short-run equilibrium. In country 1, capital per head and output per head are lower, as compared to the long-run equilibrium before shock. Foreign assets per head, however, are higher than before. More exactly, the increase in foreign assets per head equals the reduction in capital per head. The interest rate is greater than before, as is consumption per head. In country 2, on the other hand, capital per head and output per head are higher. Foreign debt per

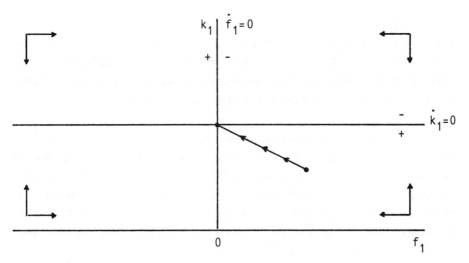

Figure 13
Technical Progress in Country 2

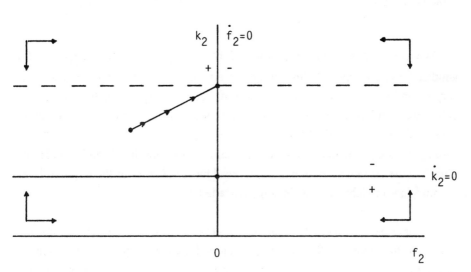

Figure 14
Technical Progress in Country 2

head is bigger, too. What is more, the change in foreign debt per head is equal in amount to the change in capital per head. The interest rate has risen, as has consumption per head. In period analysis on a yearly basis, a reallocation of the stock of capital seems not to be recessary. When savings and depreciation allowances of country 1 are invested in country 2, this may well be sufficient.

At this juncture, we come to grips with the medium run. In the phase diagrams, the streamlines indicate: In country 1, foreign assets per head decline and capital per head grows. In country 2, foreign debt per head drops and capital per head climbs. To better understand this, catch a glimpse of the current account and the trade account. In (29) $\dot{f}_1 = srf_1 - nf_1$, srf_1 symbolizes the savings out of the interest inflow, in per capita terms respectively. Compare this with $\dot{f}_1 = e_1 - nf_1$, where e_1 stands for the current account surplus per head. The comparison gives $e_1 = srf_1$. In other words, the current account surplus per head equals the savings out of the interest inflow, per head respectively. Now turn to the trade account. Let us start with $e_1 = srf_1$. The current account surplus per head can be defined as the trade surplus per head plus the interest inflow per head $e_1 = x_1 + rf_1$. And the trade deficit per head is identical to the negative value of the trade surplus per head $q_1 = -x_1$. From this one can extract $q_1 = (1-s)rf_1$. That is to say, the trade deficit per head equals the consumption out of the interest inflow, per head respectively.

What does this mean for country 1? $f_1 > 0$ implies $e_1 > 0$ and $q_1 > 0$. Put another way, country 1 holds foreign assets, so it must run a current account surplus and a trade deficit. But the current account surplus per head must stay below the required level, since foreign assets per head shrink. And what about country 2? From $f_2 < 0$ follows $e_2 < 0$ and $q_2 < 0$. Country 2 owes money to country 1, hence country 2 must incur a current account deficit and a trade surplus. Yet the current account deficit per head must fall short of the required level, because foreign debt per head is being curtailed.

As time passes away, the economy approaches a new long-run equilibrium. In each of the countries, the current account and the foreign position are balanced again. And in both countries, investment per head and capital per head stop moving. In the end, capital per head of country 1 returns to its original level. Capital per head of country 2, by way of contrast, lies well above its original level. The

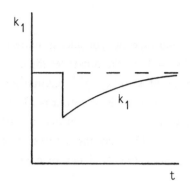

Figure 15
Capital Per Head in Country 1

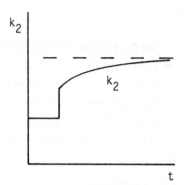

Figure 16
Capital Per Head in Country 2

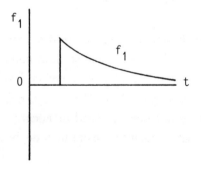

Figure 17
Foreign Assets Per Head
of Country 1

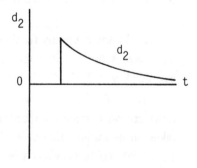

Figure 18
Foreign Debt Per Head
of Country 2

same applies to consumption per head. For the accompanying time paths see figures 15 up to 27.

To explain this from a somewhat different point of view, consider a numerical example with $\alpha = 0.2$, $n = 0.03$, $s = 0.1$ and $\varepsilon_1 = 1$. At the outset let the economy be in the steady state with $\varepsilon_2 = 1$. By virtue of $k_i = (s/n)^{1/\beta}$, capital per head is equal across countries $k_1 = k_2 = 4.50$. The same holds of output per head $y_1 = y_2 = 1.35$. The foreign positions are balanced $f_1 = f_2 = 0$. On account of $c_i = (1-s)y_i$, consumption per head is $c_1 = c_2 = 1.22$. And the interest rate amounts to $r = \alpha y_i / k_i = 0.06$. In these circumstances, the efficiency of country 2 jumps up from 1 to 2.

We proceed now to the short-run equilibrium, more precisely to period 1. $k_2 = \varepsilon_2^{1/\beta} k_1 = 2.38 k_1$ combines with $k_1 + k_2 = 9.01$ to give $k_1 = 2.67$ and $k_2 = 6.34$. Put differently, capital is reallocated in favour of country 2. Output per head of country 1 is cut back $y_1 = 1.22$, while that of country 2 is boosted $y_2 = 2.89$. Thanks to $\Delta f_1 = -\Delta k_1 = 1.84$, foreign assets per head of country 1 come into existence $f_1 = 1.84$. Similarly foreign debt per head of country 2 emerges $d_2 = 1.84$. The interest rate surges to $r = 0.09$. Due to $c_i = (1-s)(y_i + rf_i)$, consumption per head of country 1 swells to $c_1 = 1.25$, even though domestic income y_1 shrinks. The reason for this is that the interest rate goes up. Of course, consumption per head of country 2 expands markedly $c_2 = 2.45$.

Finally the economy reaches the new steady state. Capital per head of country 1 comes back to its starting point $k_1 = (s/n)^{1/\beta} = 4.50$, and so does output per head $y_1 = 1.35$. Capital per head of country 2 settles at a higher level $k_2 = (\varepsilon_2 s/n)^{1/\beta} = 10.71$, as does output per head $y_2 = 3.21$. The foreign positions are once more balanced $f_1 = f_2 = 0$. Consumption per head of country 1 takes on its initial value $c_1 = 1.22$, whereas that of country 2 more than doubles $c_2 = 2.89$. Table 14 offers a synopsis.

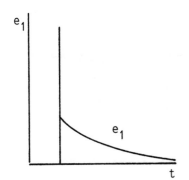

Figure 19
Current Account Surplus Per Head
of Country 1

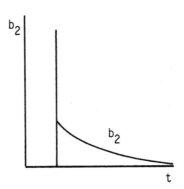

Figure 20
Current Account Deficit Per Head
of Country 2

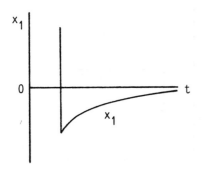

Figure 21
Trade Deficit Per Head
of Country 1

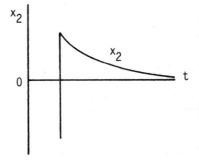

Figure 22
Trade Surplus Per Head
of Country 2

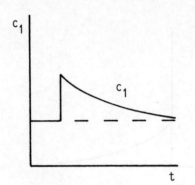

Figure 23
Consumption Per Head of Country 1

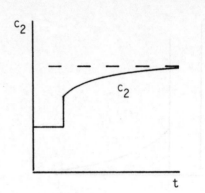

Figure 24
Consumption Per Head of Country 2

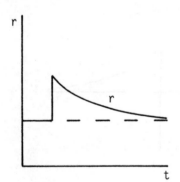

Figure 25
Interest Rate

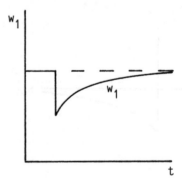

Figure 26
Wage Rate in Country 1

Table 14

Process of Adjustment (Technical Progress Abroad)

	0	1	∞
k_1	4.50	2.67	4.50
k_2	4.50	6.34	10.71
y_1	1.35	1.22	1.35
y_2	1.35	2.89	3.21
f_1	0	1.84	0
f_2	0	- 1.84	0
c_1	1.22	1.25	1.22
c_2	1.22	2.45	2.89
r	0.06	0.09	0.06

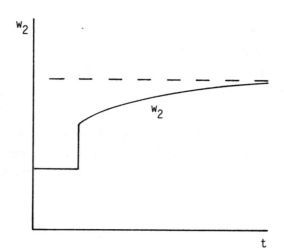

Figure 27

Wage Rate in Country 2

4. Different Rates of Labour Growth (Overlapping Generations)

4.1. Steady State

The underlying model can be represented by a system of nine equations:

$$Y_i = K_i^\alpha N_i^\beta \tag{1}$$

$$r = \alpha Y_i / K_i \tag{2}$$

$$F_i^{+1} + K_i^{+1} = \beta\delta Y_i \tag{3}$$

$$N_i^{+1} = (1+n_i)N_i \tag{4}$$

$$F_1 = -F_2 \tag{5}$$

Equation (1) has it that technology is identical across countries. Equation (3) rests on the assumption that the countries agree in time preference $\delta = \delta_1 = \delta_2$. The countries differ, however, in the rate of population growth $n_1 \neq n_2$, see equation (4). Here α, β, δ, n_i, F_i, K_i and N_i are exogenous, while r, F_i^{+1}, K_i^{+1}, N_i^{+1} and Y_i are endogenous.

From (2) follows $Y_1 / Y_2 = K_1 / K_2$. Then divide $Y_1 = K_1^\alpha N_1^\beta$ through by $Y_2 = K_2^\alpha N_2^\beta$, taking account of $Y_1 / Y_2 = K_1 / K_2$, to realize $K_1 / K_2 = N_1 / N_2$. To sum up, we get $Y_1 / Y_2 = K_1 / K_2 = N_1 / N_2$. That is to say, the international allocation of labour determines the international allocation of capital and output. In addition define at the world level $N = N_1 + N_2$, $K = K_1 + K_2$ as well as $Y = Y_1 + Y_2$. This implies $Y = K^\alpha N^\beta$, as can easily be seen. Reformulate $Y_1 = K_1^\alpha N_1^\beta$ to get $Y_1 = (K_1 / N_1)^\alpha N_1$. Likewise one can deduce $Y_2 = (K_2 / N_2)^\alpha N_2$. Then add up the last two terms $Y = Y_1 + Y_2$, noting $K/N = K_1/N_1 = K_2/N_2$, to reach $Y = (K/N)^\alpha N$ and thus $Y = K^\alpha N^\beta$. Similarly it holds $r = \alpha Y/K$. Further take the sum of (3), paying attention to $F_1 = -F_2$, to conclude $K_1^{+1} + K_2^{+1} = \beta\delta(Y_1 + Y_2)$ as well as $K^{+1} = \beta\delta Y$.

Having done this, the model simplifies to a system of five equations:

$$Y = K^{\alpha} N^{\beta} \tag{6}$$

$$K^{+1} = \beta \delta Y \tag{7}$$

$$N_1^{+1} = (1 + n_1) N_1 \tag{8}$$

$$N_2^{+1} = (1 + n_2) N_2 \tag{9}$$

$$N^{+1} = N_1^{+1} + N_2^{+1} \tag{10}$$

In this instance, K^{+1}, N^{+1}, N_1^{+1}, N_2^{+1} and Y adjust themselves appropriately.

At this point we switch to per capita terms. $Y = K^{\alpha} N^{\beta}$ can be expressed as $y = k^{\alpha}$, where $k = K/N$ denotes capital per head and $y = Y/N$ output per head. $K^{+1} = \beta \delta Y$ transforms into $(1 + n) k^{+1} = \beta \delta y$, making use of $N^{+1} = (1 + n) N$. Finally (8), (9) and (10) yield $n = (N_1 / N) n_1 + (N_2 / N) n_2$. On this foundation, the model can be characterized by a system of six equations:

$$y = k^{\alpha} \tag{11}$$

$$(1 + n) k^{+1} = \beta \delta y \tag{12}$$

$$n = (N_1 / N) n_1 + (N_2 / N) n_2 \tag{13}$$

$$N_1^{+1} = (1 + n_1) N_1 \tag{14}$$

$$N_2^{+1} = (1 + n_2) N_2 \tag{15}$$

$$N^{+1} = N_1^{+1} + N_2^{+1} \tag{16}$$

Here k^{+1}, n, y, N^{+1}, N_1^{+1} and N_2^{+1} are flexible.

In the steady state, capital per head is constant $k^{+1} = k$. Without loss of generality, let the growth rate of country 1 exceed that of country 2 $n_1 > n_2$. Then, as time goes to infinity, N_1/N converges to 1 and N_2/N to 0. As a consequence, the overall growth rate n converges to n_1. For this reason, the steady state can be described by a system of only two equations:

$$y = k^{\alpha} \tag{17}$$

$$(1 + n_1) k = \beta \delta y \tag{18}$$

At this stage, k and y are endogenous. Moreover combine (17) and (18) to attain:

$$k^\beta = \frac{\beta\delta}{1+n_1} \tag{19}$$

Evidently an increase in the saving rate enhances capital per head. An increase in the growth rate of country 1, on the other hand, depresses capital per head. And an increase in the growth rate of country 2 has no influence on capital per head (at least in the long-run).

Now $K/N = K_1/N_1 = K_2/N_2$ can be stated as $k = k_1 = k_2$. Analogously, $Y/N = Y_1/N_1 = Y_2/N_2$ can be written as $y = y_1 = y_2$. Therefore $(1+n)k^{+1} = \beta\delta y$ can be specified as $(1+n)k_1^{+1} = \beta\delta y_1$ and $(1+n)k_2^{+1} = \beta\delta y_2$, respectively. Accordingly the full model of country 1 can be captured by a system of seven equations:

$$y_1 = k_1^\alpha \tag{20}$$

$$(1+n)k_1^{+1} = \beta\delta y_1 \tag{21}$$

$$(1+n_1)f_1^{+1} + (1+n_1)k_1^{+1} = \beta\delta y_1 \tag{22}$$

$$n = (N_1/N)n_1 + (N_2/N)n_2 \tag{23}$$

$$N_1^{+1} = (1+n_1)N_1 \tag{24}$$

$$N_2^{+1} = (1+n_2)N_2 \tag{25}$$

$$N^{+1} = N_1^{+1} + N_2^{+1} \tag{26}$$

Here f_1^{+1}, k_1^{+1}, n, y_1, N^{+1}, N_1^{+1} and N_2^{+1} adjust themselves. There are as many equations as variables.

In the steady state, both foreign assets per head and capital per head come to a halt $f_1^{+1} = f_1$ and $k_1^{+1} = k_1$. Over and above that, the aggregate growth rate coincides with that of country 1 $n = n_1$, i.e. that of the fast-growing country. On these grounds, the steady state of country 1 can be caught by a system of three equations:

$$y_1 = k_1^\alpha \tag{27}$$

$$(1+n_1)k_1 = \beta\delta y_1 \tag{28}$$

$$(1+n_1)f_1 + (1+n_1)k_1 = \beta\delta y_1 \tag{29}$$

In this situation, f_1, k_1 and y_1 are flexible.

From equations (27) and (28) one can infer:

$$k_1^\beta = \frac{\beta\delta}{1+n_1} \tag{30}$$

Equations (28) and (29) produce:

$$f_1 = 0 \tag{31}$$

As an outcome, foreign assets per head of country 1 are zero. What is more, this holds irrespective of the saving rate and the growth rates (so long as $n_1 > n_2$).

In the same way, the model of country 2 can be derived:

$$y_2 = k_2^\alpha \tag{32}$$

$$(1+n)k_2^{+1} = \beta\delta y_2 \tag{33}$$

$$(1+n_2)f_2^{+1} + (1+n_2)k_2^{+1} = \beta\delta y_2 \tag{34}$$

$$n = (N_1/N)n_1 + (N_2/N)n_2 \tag{35}$$

$$N_1^{+1} = (1+n_1)N_1 \tag{36}$$

$$N_2^{+1} = (1+n_2)N_2 \tag{37}$$

$$N^{+1} = N_1^{+1} + N_2^{+1} \tag{38}$$

Here f_2^{+1}, k_2^{+1}, n, y_2, N^{+1}, N_1^{+1} and N_2^{+1} are endogenous.

In the steady state, foreign assets per head and capital per head do no longer move $f_2^{+1} = f_2$ and $k_2^{+1} = k_2$. Beyond that, the overall growth rate agrees with the growth rate of country 1. Correspondingly the steady state of country 2 can be encapsulated in a system of three equations:

$$y_2 = k_2^\alpha \tag{39}$$

$$(1+n_1)k_2 = \beta\delta y_2 \tag{40}$$

$$(1+n_2)f_2 + (1+n_2)k_2 = \beta\delta y_2 \tag{41}$$

At this stage, f_2, k_2 and y_2 adjust themselves.

From equations (39) and (40), one can extract:

$$k_2^\beta = \frac{\beta\delta}{1+n_1} \tag{42}$$

This is equivalent to the findings for country 1. Equations (40) and (41) provide $f_2 = (n_1 - n_2)k_2 / (1+n_2)$. Besides substitute (42) to accomplish:

$$f_2 = \frac{n_1 - n_2}{1+n_2} \left(\frac{\beta\delta}{1+n_1} \right)^{1/\beta} \tag{43}$$

As a corollary, we have $f_2 > 0$, since $n_1 > n_2$. That means, country 2 will be a creditor. The other way round, country 1 will be a debtor. An increase in the saving rate raises foreign assets per head of country 2. The same applies to an increase in the growth rate of country 1, at least locally. Conversely, an increase in the growth rate of country 2 lowers foreign assets per head of country 2.

The conclusion that country 1 will be a debtor at first sight appears to clash with $f_1 = 0$. To make this argument clear, reformulate $F_1 = -F_2$ as:

$$\frac{F_1}{N_1} = -\frac{N_2}{N_1} \frac{F_2}{N_2} \tag{44}$$

As time goes to infinity, both N_1 and N_2 grow without limits. In this process, N_2/N_1 declines to zero. The foreign assets of country 2 become very large (i.e. plus infinity), whereas the foreign assets of country 1 become very small (i.e. minus infinity). F_2/N_2 converges to the right-hand side of (43), as has been demonstrated above. Then, by virtue of (44), F_1/N_1 converges to zero. Hence the story told above is consistent.

In summary, the fast-growing country will be a debtor with foreign debt per head equal to zero. The slow-growing country, on the other hand, will be a creditor with foreign assets per head well above zero. Table 15 presents an overview.

Table 15
Long-Run Effects (Two Countries)

	δ	n_1	n_2
k_1	+	–	0
k_2	+	–	0
d_1	0	0	0
f_2	+	+	–

4.2. Process of Adjustment

The current section is devoted to two subjects, stability analysis and transitional dynamics. At first we shall probe into the stability of country 1. The model can be condensed to a system of two difference equations:

$$f_1^{+1} = g_1(f_1, k_1) \tag{1}$$
$$k_1^{+1} = h_1(f_1, k_1) \tag{2}$$

Let us begin with f_1^{+1}. Confront (21) and (22) from the preceding sections, observing (20), to verify:

$$f_1^{+1} = -\frac{(n_1 - n)\beta\delta k_1^\alpha}{(1+n)(1+n_1)} \tag{3}$$

Obviously an increase in k_1 reduces f_1^{+1}. In the steady state, foreign assets per head are uniform $f_1^{+1} = f_1$. This involves:

$$f_1 = -\frac{(n_1 - n)\beta\delta k_1^\alpha}{(1+n)(1+n_1)} \tag{4}$$

For ease of exposition, focus on the limiting point $n = n_1$, which gives $f_1 = 0$. Figure 28 shows the vertical ff demarcation line.

We come now to k_1^{+1}. Insert (20) into (21) from the preceding section:

$$k_1^{+1} = \frac{\beta\delta k_1^\alpha}{1+n} \tag{5}$$

Differentiate (5) for k_1 and evaluate the derivative at the steady state with $n = n_1$ as well as $k_1^\beta = \beta\delta/(1+n_1)$ to ascertain:

$$\frac{\partial k_1^{+1}}{\partial k_1} = \alpha < 1 \tag{6}$$

In the steady state, capital per head stops moving $k_1^{+1} = k_1$. Setting $n = n_1$, this yields:

$$k_1^\beta = \frac{\beta\delta}{1+n_1} \tag{7}$$

Figure 28 portrays the horizontal kk demarcation line. The directional arrows indicate that the steady state will be stable.

What about the stability of country 2? The model can be written down as a system of two difference equations:

$$f_2^{+1} = g_2(f_2, k_2) \tag{8}$$
$$k_2^{+1} = h_2(f_2, k_2) \tag{9}$$

Let us start with f_2^{+1}. Eliminate k_2^{+1} in (34) with the help of (33), taking into account (32), to arrive at:

$$f_2^{+1} = \frac{(n - n_2)\beta\delta k_2^{\alpha}}{(1+n)(1+n_2)} \tag{10}$$

So a rise in k_2 lifts f_2^{+1}. In the steady state, foreign assets per head come to a standstill $f_2^{+1} = f_2$. This supplies:

$$f_2 = \frac{(n - n_2)\beta\delta k_2^{\alpha}}{(1+n)(1+n_2)} \tag{11}$$

Figure 29 depicts the upward sloping ff demarcation line. In full analogy to country 1 the horizontal kk demarcation line can be obtained. The steady state will be stable, as can be learnt from the phase diagram.

At this point we leave stability analysis and turn to the process of adjustment. Particularly we study the dynamic effects of an increase in the rate of labour growth in country 1. Figure 30 visualizes the exogenous time paths of the rates of labour growth in countries 1 and 2, respectively, as well as the endogenous time path of the rate of labour growth at world level.

First have a look at capital per head in country 1. The equation of motion is given by (5). Initially capital per head does not change $k_1^{+1} = k_1$. Then the rate of labour growth in country 1 goes up. In the short run, this raises the rate of labour growth at world level, thereby lowering capital per head in the subsequent period. In the medium run, the reduction in capital per head this period leads to a reduction in capital per head next period. Simultaneously the rate of labour growth at world level continues to rise, which reinforces the downward pressure on capi-

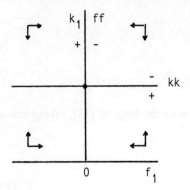

Figure 28

Different Rates of Labour Growth

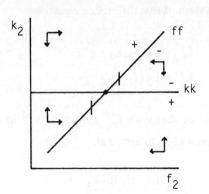

Figure 29

Different Rates of Labour Growth

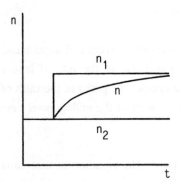

Figure 30

Increase in Labour Growth
of Country 1

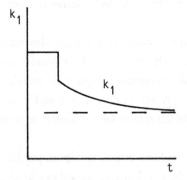

Figure 31

Capital Per Head in Country 1
(Country 2)

tal per head in the subsequent periods. Figure 31 plots how capital per head in country 1 develops. Of course the time pattern of capital per head in country 2 is isomorphic.

Second consider foreign assets per head in country 1. The equation of motion is given by (3). At the beginning foreign assets per head are invariant. What is more, due to $n_1 = n_2$, the foreign position is balanced $f_1^{+1} = f_1 = 0$. Now the rate of labour growth in country 1 increases. In the short run, this diminishes foreign assets per head in the subsequent period, so they become negative. In the medium run, the drop in capital per head this period causes a lift in foreign assets per head next period. At the same time, the rate of labour growth at world level keeps on rising, thus augmenting foreign assets per head even further. Figure 32 graphs how foreign assets per head in country 1 evolve.

Third regard foreign assets per head in country 2. The equation of motion is given by (10). Originally foreign assets per head do not move $f_2^{+1} = f_2 = 0$. Then the rate of labour growth in country 1 jumps up. In the short run, this enhances the rate of labour growth at world level, which boosts foreign assets per head in the subsequent period, hence they become positive. In the medium run, the rate of labour growth at world level continues to rise, which brings up foreign assets per head once more. For the time path see figure 33.

Next transitional dynamics will be discussed coherently. At the start, let the economy be in the steady state with $n_1 = n_2$. The foreign positions are balanced. In each of the countries, capital per head is uniform. Figure 34 represents country 1, and figure 35 country 2. The steady state is marked by the intersection of the ff and kk lines. Against this background, the rate of labour growth in country 1 increases. In figure 34, the kk line shifts downwards. In figure 35, the ff line shifts to the right, and the kk line shifts downwards. In the short run, as a reaction, capital flows from country 2 to country 1. Therefore country 1 becomes a debtor, and country 2 a creditor. In both countries, capital per head declines. In the medium run, foreign debt per head of country 1 decumulates. Foreign assets per head of country 2 however accumulate, which at first sight seems to be somewhat surprising. In each of the countries, capital per head keeps on falling. The streamlines in the phase diagrams indicate how the countries move. Eventually the economy reaches a new steady state. Foreign debt per head of country 1 has

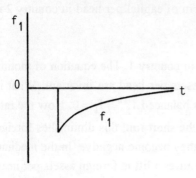

Figure 32
Foreign Debt Per Head
of Country 1

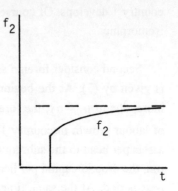

Figure 33
Foreign Assets Per Head
of Country 2

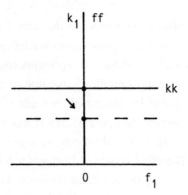

Figure 34
Increase in Labour Growth
of Country 1

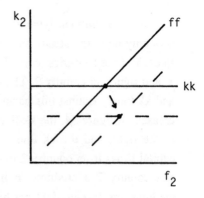

Figure 35
Increase in Labour Growth
of Country 1

disappeared from the scene $d_1 = 0$, while foreign assets per head of country 2 are still in existence $f_2 > 0$.

Last but not least, to illustrate this, take a numerical example. It is convenient to draw here on the Solow model. As a result one gets the foreign asset ratio of country 2 $f_2 / y_2 = (n_1 - n_2)s / (n_2 - \alpha n_1)n_1$. Posit $\alpha = 0.2$, $n_1 = n_2 = 0.03$ and s $= 0.1$ to calculate $f_2 / y_2 = 0$. Now the rate of labour growth in country 1 increases to 0.04. As a response, the foreign asset ratio of country 2 rises to 1.14.

CHAPTER III. IMPERFECT CAPITAL MOBILITY

1. Solow Model (Fixed Debt Ratio)

1.1. Steady State

In the model with perfect capital mobility, small differences in saving rates across countries lead to very large foreign debt ratios (foreign asset ratios, for that matter). This result, however, seems not to be consistent with empirical evidence. Feldstein and Horioka (1980) demonstrated that investment rates are highly correlated with saving rates. In the United States, for instance, foreign debt is nearly 10% of GDP. And in Germany, foreign assets reached a maximum of about 20% of GDP.

How can this puzzle be solved? The answer seems to be that capital mobility is rather imperfect, cf. Feldstein (1994, 1995). International credit rationing causes a segmentation of capital markets. There is a high risk in lending abroad as contrasted with lending at home. On the one hand there is the policy risk, which includes the risk of capital controls, the risk of convertibility restrictions and the default risk on sovereign debt. On the other hand there is the currency risk, consisting mainly of devaluations and depreciations. Therefore lenders have a strong incentive to impose constraints on lending abroad.

In the current chapter, imperfect capital mobility will be allowed for in either of two ways. First, the foreign debt of a country must not exceed a critical level, expressed in terms of its capital stock as a collateral (maximum feasible debt - capital ratio). And second, the interest rate to be paid by the borrowing country to the lending country is an increasing function of the debt-capital ratio. What will be the implications of this for economic growth?

As a point of departure, consider a small open economy with perfect capital mobility, cf. section 1.2. in chapter I. The model is composed of three equations:

$$y = k^\alpha \tag{1}$$

$$r^* = \alpha y / k \tag{2}$$

$$\dot{d} = nk - s(y - r^*d) - nd \tag{3}$$

Here r^* denotes the foreign interest rate which is assumed to be constant. α, d, n, r^* and s are exogenous, while $\dot{d}$, k and y are endogenous. Equations (1) and (2) produce:

$$k = (\alpha / r^*)^{1/\beta} \tag{4}$$

$$y = (\alpha / r^*)^{\alpha/\beta} \tag{5}$$

In the steady state, foreign debt per head does not move any longer $\dot{d} = 0$. Accordingly the steady state can be written down as a system of three equations:

$$y = k^{\alpha} \tag{6}$$

$$r^* = \alpha y / k \tag{7}$$

$$nd = nk - s(y - r^*d) \tag{8}$$

Here α, n, r^* and s are given, whereas d, k and y adjust themselves. Equation (8) yields:

$$d = \frac{nk - sy}{n - r^* s} \tag{9}$$

We come now to a small open economy with imperfect capital mobility. Let the country in question be a debtor. Suppose again a Cobb-Douglas technology $Y = K^{\alpha}N^{\beta}$. The interest rate corresponds to the marginal product of capital $r = \alpha Y/K$. Here r symbolizes the domestic interest rate, which is variable by assumption. Let labour grow at the natural rate $\dot{N} = nN$.

Moreover have a look at both capital and debt dynamics. $\bar{r}$ stands for the interest rate paid on foreign debt D, so the interest outflow amounts to $\bar{r}D$. It is safe to posit $\bar{r} \geq r^*$. The income of domestic residents consists of factor income, diminished by the interest outflow $Y - \bar{r}D$. Domestic residents save a certain fraction of their income $S = s(Y - \bar{r}D)$. Investment can be financed from two sources, savings and foreign borrowing $I = S + B$. Investment, in turn, adds to the stock of capital $\dot{K} = I$. Likewise, foreign borrowing adds to foreign debt $\dot{D} = B$. From this one can conclude $\dot{K} = s(Y - \bar{r}D) + \dot{D}$. m denotes the maximum feasible debt-capital ratio (in short, the maximum debt ratio). Let be m < 1. In addition, let the constraint be operative $D = mK$ and $\dot{D} = m\dot{K}$. Substitute this into $\dot{K} = s(Y - \bar{r}D) + \dot{D}$ to get $(1 - m)\dot{K} = s(Y - m\bar{r}K)$. The basic idea is that an increase in the stock of capital permits the country in question to raise more loans abroad, thereby increasing its stock of capital once more, and so on.

On these grounds, the model can be characterized by a system of four equations:

$$Y = K^{\alpha}N^{\beta} \tag{10}$$

$$r = \alpha Y / K \tag{11}$$

$$(1 - m)\dot{K} = s(Y - m\bar{r}K) \tag{12}$$

$$\dot{N} = nN \tag{13}$$

Within this framework α, β, m, n, $\bar{r}$, s, K and N are fixed, while r, $\dot{K}$, $\dot{N}$ and Y are flexible.

It is useful to carry out the investigation in per capita terms. Take the time derivative of capital per head $\dot{k} = \dot{K}/N - K\dot{N}/N^2$. Then get rid of $\dot{K}$ by means of $(1 - m)\dot{K} = s(Y - m\bar{r}K)$ to achieve $(1 - m)\dot{k} = s(y - m\bar{r}k) - (1 - m)nk$. Thus the model can be represented by a system of three equations:

$$y = k^{\alpha} \tag{14}$$

$$r = \alpha y / k \tag{15}$$

$$(1 - m)\dot{k} = s(y - m\bar{r}k) - (1 - m)nk \tag{16}$$

Here α, k, m, n, $\bar{r}$ and s are exogenous, whereas $\dot{k}$, r and y are endogenous.

In the steady state, capital per head is invariant $\dot{k} = 0$. For that reason, the steady state can be described by a system of three equations:

$$y = k^{\alpha} \tag{17}$$

$$r = \alpha y / k \tag{18}$$

$$(1-m)nk = s(y - m\bar{r}k) \tag{19}$$

In these circumstances α, m, n, $\bar{r}$ and s are given, while k, r and y adjust themselves.

We examine next the major properties of the steady state. From (17) and (19) follows:

$$k^\beta = \frac{s}{m\bar{r}s + n - mn} \tag{20}$$

Obviously, an increase in the saving rate raises capital per head. An increase in the growth rate lowers capital per head. An increase in the maximum debt ratio enhances capital per head, granted $n > \bar{r}s$. And an increase in the foreign interest rate $\bar{r}$ depresses capital per head. This is in remarkable contrast to the results obtained under perfect capital mobility. There an increase in the saving rate leaves no impact on capital per head. The same holds for an increase in the growth rate. And an increase in the foreign interest rate reduces capital per head, as under imperfect capital mobility.

Moreover we have:

$$d = mk \tag{21}$$

Judging by this, a rise in the saving rate brings up foreign debt per head. A rise in the growth rate cuts back foreign debt per head. A rise in the maximum debt ratio lifts foreign debt per head. And a rise in the foreign interest rate pulls down foreign debt per head. Again this clearly differs from the conclusions drawn under perfect capital mobility. There a rise in the saving rate leads to a fall in foreign debt per head. A rise in the growth rate augments foreign debt per head. And a rise in the foreign interest rate diminishes foreign debt per head (which is quite the same as under imperfect capital mobility).

Besides regard the domestic interest rate. (17), (18) and (19) combine to give:

$$r = \frac{\alpha(m\bar{r}s + n - mn)}{s} \qquad (22)$$

An increase in the saving rate lowers the domestic interest rate. An increase in the growth rate raises the domestic interest rate. An increase in the maximum debt ratio curtails the domestic interest rate. And an increase in the foreign interest rate enhances the domestic interest rate. Further contemplate the current account deficit per head:

$$b = nd \qquad (23)$$

A rise in the saving rate expands foreign debt per head and thus the current account deficit per head. A rise in the growth rate contracts foreign debt per head, so the effect on the current account deficit per head will be ambiguous. A rise in the maximum debt ratio drives up foreign debt per head and hence the current account deficit per head. And a rise in the foreign interest rate reduces foreign debt per head and thereby the current account deficit per head. At last catch a glimpse of the trade surplus per head:

$$x = (\bar{r} - n)d \qquad (24)$$

Still let be $\bar{r} > n$. A lift in the saving rate boosts the trade surplus per head. A lift in the growth rate cuts back the trade surplus per head. A lift in the maximum debt ratio pushes up the trade surplus per head. And a lift in the foreign interest rate can exert upward or downward pressure on the trade surplus per head.

In summary, an increase in the saving rate augments both capital per head and output per head. It raises foreign debt per head and lowers the domestic interest rate. An increase in the growth rate diminishes capital per head and output per head. It reduces foreign debt per head and bids up the domestic interest rate. And an increase in the maximum debt ratio expands both capital per head and output per head. It enhances foreign debt per head and depresses the domestic interest rate. This is in sharp contradistinction to the findings under perfect capital mobility. There an increase in the saving rate has no influence on either capital per head or output per head. It contracts foreign debt per head, while the domestic interest rate remains unchanged. Table 16 displays these consequences.

Table 16

Long-Run Effects (Imperfect Capital Mobility)

	s	n	m	$\bar{r}$
$\dot{k}$	+	−	+	−
y	+	−	+	−
d	+	−	+	−
r	−	+	−	+

The next point refers to stability. The model can be compressed to a single differential equation $\dot{k} = g(k)$. Insert (14) into (16) to get:

$$(1-m)\dot{k} = s(k^{\alpha} - m\bar{r}k) - (1-m)nk \qquad (25)$$

Then differentiate (25) for k and evaluate the derivative at the steady state with (20) to realize:

$$\frac{\partial \dot{k}}{\partial k} < 0 \qquad (26)$$

As an outcome, the steady state proves to be stable. For the phase diagram see figure 1.

For the remainder of this section we shall deal with regime switching. Let j symbolize the actual debt ratio, given perfect capital mobility (i.e. the debt ratio that would occur under perfect capital mobility). Accordingly there exist two possible regimes, j < m and j > m. If j < m, then the contraint is not binding d/k <

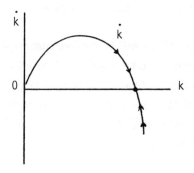

Figure 1
Phase Diagram

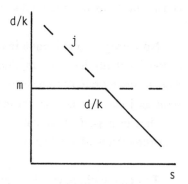

Figure 2
Saving Rate and
Debt-Capital Ratio

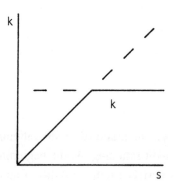

Figure 3
Saving Rate and
Capital Per Head

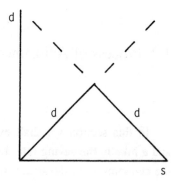

Figure 4
Saving Rate and
Foreign Debt Per Head

m, so we have perfect capital mobility. The other way round, if j > m, then the constraint is indeed binding d/k = m, hence we get imperfect capital mobility.

Now imagine a reduction in the saving rate. What will be the long-run implications? Initially let be j < m, thus we have perfect capital mobility. Then assume that the saving rate declines step by step. Because of this, j rises step by step. As soon as j exceeds m, the constraint becomes binding. That means, the regime switches to imperfect capital mobility. In this sense, figures 2 up to 5 show the long-run effects of a reduction in the saving rate.

To begin with, have a look at the debt-capital ratio in figure 2. Evidently two phases are to be distinguished. During the first phase, the reduction in the saving rate increases the debt-capital ratio. During the second phase, however, the debt-capital ratio does no longer respond. We turn next to capital per head, cf. figure 3. During the first phase, capital per head is fixed. But during the second phase, it drops. Figure 4 portrays the reaction of foreign debt per head. During the first phase, foreign debt per head rises. Conversely, during the second phase, it falls. Figure 5 visualizes the domestic interest rate. During the first phase, the domestic interest rate does not change, being pegged at the level of the foreign interest rate. Yet during the second phase, the domestic interest rate goes up.

1.2. Process of Adjustment

In this section we shall examine two shocks, international credit rationing and a hike in the saving rate. Let us start with credit rationing. At the beginning, the economy is in the steady state. There exists perfect capital mobility. Capital per head and foreign debt per head are uniform. Then, all of a sudden, lenders impose a constraint on foreign borrowing. More exactly, foreign debt must not exceed a critical level, expressed in terms of the capital stock. In addition, let the maximum feasible debt-capital ratio be binding. Instantaneously, this measure reduces foreign debt per head and thus capital per head. Properly speaking, the reduction in capital per head equals the reduction in foreign debt per head. The fall

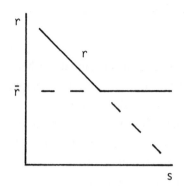

Figure 5
Saving Rate and
Domestic Interest Rate

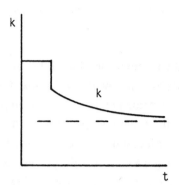

Figure 6
Capital Per Head
(International Credit Rationing)

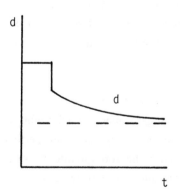

Figure 7
Foreign Debt Per Head

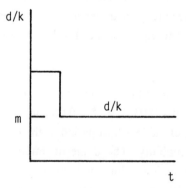

Figure 8
Debt-Capital Ratio

in capital per head induces a fall in output per head and income per head. That is why consumption per head, savings per head and investment per head come down.

In the medium run, due to the drop in investment per head, capital per head decumulates. And owing to $d = mk$, foreign debt per head declines too. Output per head, income per head and consumption per head come down even further. In the end, the economy approaches a new steady state. Of course, capital has become imperfectly mobile. Capital per head and foreign debt per head stop to adjust. Taking the sum over the process as a whole, capital, output, foreign debt and consumption have settled down at lower levels, in per capita terms, respectively. Figures 6 till 9 keep track of the principal variables.

Here we leave the introduction of credit rationing and go on to an increase in the saving rate. Originally the economy is in the long-run equilibrium. Capital per head and foreign debt per head do not vary. Then, abruptly, the saving rate moves up. In the short run, this lowers consumption per head and raises investment per head. In the intermediate run, the rise in investment per head leads to the growth of capital per head. By virtue of $d = mk$, this is accompanied by the growth of foreign debt per head, which in turn feeds back on the growth of capital per head. Output per head, income per head and consumption per head improve. With the lapse of time, the economy gravitates to a new long-run equilibrium. Capital per head and foreign debt per head do no longer change. To summarize, capital per head and foreign debt per head went up. Figures 10 until 12 trace out the time paths.

To explain this in greater detail, consider a numerical example with $\alpha = 0.2$, $\beta = 0.8$, $n = 0.03$, $\bar{r} = r^* = 0.06$ and $s = 0.06$. First regard international credit rationing, cf. table 17. In period 0, the economy is in the steady state with perfect capital mobility. The domestic interest rate matches the foreign interest rate. Then, in period 1, foreigners impose a constraint on domestic borrowing $m = 0.1$. To simplify matters, assume that foreigners abruptly withdraw their capital $\Delta k = \Delta d$. Hence $k_1 - k_0 = d_1 - d_0$ and $d_1 = mk_1$ furnish $k_1 = (k_0 - d_0)/(1-m)$. Therefore consumption per head drops by 1.8%. And the domestic interest rate surpasses the foreign interest rate. Ultimately the economy arrives at a steady state with $m = 0.1$. Consumption per head has deteriorated by 2.2%.

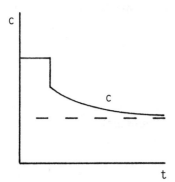

Figure 9
Consumption Per Head

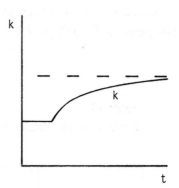

Figure 10
Capital Per Head
(Increase in Saving Rate)

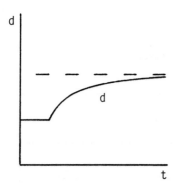

Figure 11
Foreign Debt Per Head

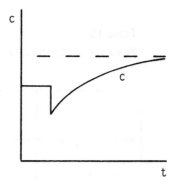

Figure 12
Consumption Per Head

126

Second contemplate an increase in the saving rate, cf. table 18. In period 0, the economy is in the steady state with m = 0.1. Then, spontaneously, the saving rate jumps up from 6% to 7%.

Table 17
Process of Adjustment (International Credit Rationing)

	0	1	∞
k	4.504	2.730	2.669
y	1.351	1.222	1.217
d	2.047	0.273	0.267
c	1.155	1.134	1.129
r	0.060	0.090	0.091

Table 18
Process of Adjustment (Increase in Saving Rate)

	0	1	∞
k	2.669	2.682	3.227
y	1.217	1.218	1.264
d	0.267	0.268	0.323
c	1.129	1.118	1.158

2. Overlapping Generations

2.1. Fixed Debt Ratio

As a base of comparison, take a small open economy with perfect capital mobility, cf. sections 1.2 and 2 in chapter I. The model consists of three equations:

$$y = k^{\alpha} \tag{1}$$
$$r* = \alpha y / k \tag{2}$$
$$(1+n)d_{+1} = (1+n)k - \beta\delta y \tag{3}$$

Here $r* = \text{const}$ denotes the foreign interest rate. Equation (3) states that foreign debt is the excess of capital over assets. α, β, δ, n and $r*$ are exogenous, while d_{+1}, k and y are endogenous. From (1) and (2) one can gain $k = (\alpha/r*)^{1/\beta}$ and $y = (\alpha/r*)^{\alpha/\beta}$.

In the steady state, foreign debt per head is invariant $d_{+1} = d$. Correspondingly the steady state can be captured by a system of three equations:

$$y = k^{\alpha} \tag{4}$$
$$r* = \alpha y / k \tag{5}$$
$$(1+n)d = (1+n)k - \beta\delta y \tag{6}$$

In this condition α, β, δ, n and $r*$ are given, whereas d, k and y adjust themselves appropriately. (6) provides foreign debt per head:

$$d = k - \frac{\beta\delta y}{1+n} \tag{7}$$

We proceed now to a small open economy with imperfect capital mobility. m symbolizes the maximum feasible debt-capital ratio (maximum debt ratio). Let be $m < 1$. In addition, let the constraint be operative $d = mk$. The stock of capital can be financed by two instruments, by assets and foreign debt $(1 + n)k_{+1} = \beta\delta y + (1 + n)d_{+1}$. Paying attention to $d = mk$, this can be reformulated as $(1 - m)(1 + n)k_{+1} = \beta\delta y$. The basic idea is again that an increase in the stock of capital permits the country in question to raise more loans abroad, thereby reinforcing the increase in the stock of capital etc. Thus the model is made up of three equations:

$$y = k^\alpha \tag{8}$$

$$r = \alpha y / k \tag{9}$$

$$(1 - m)(1 + n)k_{+1} = \beta\delta y \tag{10}$$

Here r stands for the domestic interest rate which is assumed to be variable. α, β, δ, k, m and n are fixed, while k_{+1}, r and y are flexible.

In the steady state, capital per head ceases to move $k_{+1} = k$. Therefore the steady state can be caught by a system of three equations:

$$y = k^\alpha \tag{11}$$

$$r = \alpha y / k \tag{12}$$

$$(1 - m)(1 + n)k = \beta\delta y \tag{13}$$

At this stage α, β, δ, m and n are exogenous, whereas k, r and y are endogenous.

What are the salient features of the steady state? From (11) and (13) one can deduce:

$$k^\beta = \frac{\beta\delta}{(1 - m)(1 + n)} \tag{14}$$

An increase in the saving rate raises capital per head. An increase in the growth rate lowers capital per head. And an increase in the maximum debt ratio lifts capital per head. This is in sharp contrast to the findings under perfect capital mobility. Moreover foreign debt per head amounts to $d = mk$. A rise in the saving rate leads to a rise in capital per head and hence in foreign debt per head. In other words, the increase in capital per head is greater than the increase in assets per head. A rise in the growth rate brings about a fall in foreign debt per head. And a rise in the maximum debt ratio causes a rise in foreign debt per head. This clearly differs from the conclusions drawn under perfect capital mobility.

Next we shed some light on the domestic interest rate. From (11), (12) and (14) one can infer:

$$r = \frac{\alpha(1-m)(1+n)}{\beta\delta} \qquad (15)$$

An increase in the saving rate reduces the domestic interest rate. An increase in the growth rate boosts the domestic interest rate. And an increase in the maximum debt ratio cuts back the domestic interest rate. In this connection, what interest rate $\bar{r}$ do domestic residents pay to foreigners? We started from the premise that the foreign interest rate is constant and the domestic interest rate variable. Of course, the domestic interest rate lies well above the foreign interest rate, since the constraint $d = mk$ is binding. So $\bar{r}$ will be situated in between $r^* \leq \bar{r} \leq r$. What is more, the size of $\bar{r}$ does not affect the results obtained so far.

Table 19
Long-Run Effects (Imperfect Capital Mobility)

	δ	n	m
k	+	−	+
y	+	−	+
d	+	−	+
r	−	+	−

In summary, an increase in the saving rate pushes up both capital per head and output per head. It enhances foreign debt per head and depresses the domestic interest rate. This is in opposition to the outcome under perfect capital mobility. Table 19 contains a synopsis.

Another point refers to stability. The model can be encapsulated in a single difference equation $k_{+1} = g(k)$. Equations (8) and (10) yield:

$$k_{+1} = \frac{\beta \delta k^{\alpha}}{(1-m)(1+n)} \tag{16}$$

Differentiate (16) for k and evaluate the ensuing term at the steady state with (14) to verify:

$$\frac{\partial k_{+1}}{\partial k} = \alpha < 1 \tag{17}$$

That is to say, the steady state turns out to be stable. Thanks to (16), figure 13 displays k_{+1} as a function of k. In the steady state, the motion of capital per head comes to a halt, see point 1. The step line plots the transition from point 0 to point 1.

At this juncture, we address the dynamic consequences of two distinct shocks, an increase in the saving rate and an increase in the maximum debt ratio. First have a look at the savings shock. Initially the economy is in the steady state. Capital per head and foreign debt per head are uniform. Then the saving rate goes up. In the phase diagram, the k_{+1} line shifts upwards, cf. figure 14. In the short run, with a one-period delay, the shock raises capital per head. By virtue of $d = mk$, this pushes up foreign debt per head, so capital per head rises even further. In the medium run, the increase in income per head is accompanied by an increase in savings per head, thus capital per head continues to grow. And due to $d = mk$, foreign debt per head keeps on growing, which speeds up the expansion of capital per head. Asymptotically the economy converges to a new steady state. Capital per head and foreign debt per head do not change any more. The arrows in figure 14 indicate the process of adjustment.

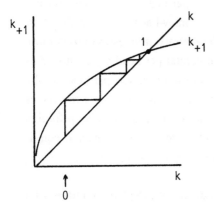

Figure 13
Phase Diagram

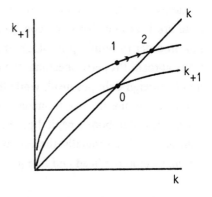

Figure 14
Increase in Saving Rate

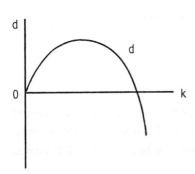

Figure 15
Capital Per Head and
Foreign Debt Per Head

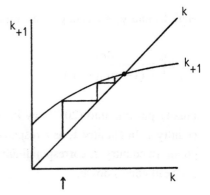

Figure 16
Phase Diagram

Second consider a shock in the maximum debt ratio. At the beginning the economy is in the permanent equilibrium. Capital per head and foreign debt per head are invariant. Now the constraint becomes somewhat relaxed. In the short run, in order to build up its stock of capital, the country in question raises more loans abroad. Properly speaking, the addition to capital per head equals the addition to foreign debt per head, while there is no addition to assets per head. In the intermediate run, the rise in income per head is associated with a rise in savings per head, which boosts capital per head. Owing to $d = mk$, this drives up foreign debt per head. Eventually the economy draws close to a new permanent equilibrium. Capital per head and foreign debt per head stop to pile up.

Last but not least, a few remarks will be made concerning two countries with imperfect capital mobility. Posit $\delta_1 < \delta_2$, hence country 1 will be a debtor and country 2 a creditor. Let the constraint imposed upon country 1 be binding $d_1 = m_1 k_1$. Besides assume $N_1 = N_2$. Along the same lines as before, the steady state can be represented by a system of four equations:

$$y_i = k_i^{\alpha} \tag{18}$$

$$(1+n)k_1 = \beta\delta_1 y_1 + (1+n)m_1 k_1 \tag{19}$$

$$(1+n)k_2 = \beta\delta_2 y_2 - (1+n)m_1 k_1 \tag{20}$$

Here k_i and y_i are endogenous. Equations (18) and (19) give:

$$k_1^{\beta} = \frac{\beta\delta_1}{(1-m_1)(1+n)} \tag{21}$$

Finally put this into (20). Now imagine that country 2 relaxes the constraint on country 1. In country 1, as a response, capital per head and foreign debt per head go up. In country 2, correspondingly, foreign assets per head go up, while capital per head comes down.

2.2. Endogenous Interest Rate

The analysis will be conducted within the framework of a small open economy. Let the country be a debtor. Suppose that the interest rate to be paid on foreign debt is an increasing function of the debt-capital ratio $r = a + bd/k$. Here r at the same time denotes the domestic interest rate, a and b are positive constants, and d/k is the debt-capital ratio. Besides, a can be viewed as the riskless rate of foreign interest $a = r^* = $ const. The underlying notion is that an increase in the debt-capital ratio bids up the interest rate to be paid on foreign debt, thereby curbing capital per head. Take for instance a reduction in the saving rate. This shock augments the debt-capital ratio and the interest rate, thus diminishing capital per head.

Pursuing the same approach as before, the model can be described by a system of four equations:

$$y = k^{\alpha} \tag{1}$$
$$r = \alpha y / k \tag{2}$$
$$r = a + bd / k \tag{3}$$
$$(1+n)k_{+1} - (1+n)d_{+1} = \beta\delta y \tag{4}$$

Here α, β, δ, a, b, d, k and n are exogenous, while d_{+1}, k_{+1}, r and y are endogenous.

Accordingly the steady state can be written down as follows:

$$y = k^{\alpha} \tag{5}$$
$$r = \alpha y / k \tag{6}$$
$$r = a + bd / k \tag{7}$$
$$(1+n)k = \beta\delta y + (1+n)d \tag{8}$$

In these circumstances α, β, δ, a, b and n are given, whereas d, k, r and y adjust themselves.

From (5), (6) and (7) one can infer:

$$d = \frac{\alpha k^{\alpha} - ak}{b} \tag{9}$$

Beyond that dispense with y and d in (8) by means of (5) and (9) to ascertain:

$$k^{\beta} = \frac{\beta \delta b}{(a+b)(1+n)} + \frac{\alpha}{a+b} \tag{10}$$

Therefore an increase in the saving rate pushes up capital per head. An increase in the growth rate pulls down capital per head. And the same applies to an increase in a or b, see below. This is in contradistinction to the findings under perfect capital mobility. More exactly we get $\partial k/\partial b < 0$, provided $a < \alpha(1 + n)/\beta\delta$. Here a symbolizes the riskless foreign interest rate, and $\alpha(1 + n)/\beta\delta$ is the domestic interest rate that would hold in the state of autarky. The proof goes as follows. Combine $r = \alpha y/k$ and $(1 + n)k = \beta\delta y$ to realize $r = \alpha(1 + n)/\beta\delta$. For a debtor country the condition just mentioned will be satisfied. Relying on (9), figure 15 shows foreign debt per head as a function of capital per head. An increase in the saving rate brings up capital per head. Foreign debt per head, on the other hand, may either rise or fall.

In summary, an increase in the saving rate lowers the debt-capital ratio and the interest rate, thereby raising capital per head. Conversely, an increase in the growth rate enhances the debt-capital ratio and the interest rate, which depresses capital per head. This deviates from perfect capital mobility.

Coming to an end, we probe into stability. The model can be condensed to a single difference equation $k_{+1} = g(k)$. Substitute (1) into (4) and rearrange $k_{+1} = \beta\delta k^{\alpha}/(1+n) + d_{+1}$. Then eliminate d_{+1} by making use of (9) to verify:

$$\left(1 + \frac{a}{b}\right)k_{+1} - \frac{\alpha}{b}k_{+1}^{\alpha} = \frac{\beta\delta k^{\alpha}}{1+n} \tag{11}$$

On these grounds, figure 16 visualizes capital per head next period as a function of capital per head this period. The phase diagram demonstrates that the steady state will be stable.

3. Infinite Horizon (Fixed Debt Ratio)

Let technology be of the Cobb-Douglas variety $Y = K^{\alpha} N^{\beta}$. The domestic interest rate harmonizes with the marginal product of capital $r = \alpha Y/K$. Domestic output serves for consumption, investment and net exports $Y = C + I + X$. Investment in turn adds to the stock of capital $\dot{K} = I$. Domestic residents pay the interest rate $\bar{r}$ on foreign debt D, so the interest outflow amounts to $\bar{r}D$. The current account deficit augments foreign debt $\dot{D} = \bar{r}D - X$. And labour grows at a constant rate $\dot{N} = nN$. In per capita terms, this can be expressed as follows:

$$y = k^{\alpha} \tag{1}$$

$$r = \alpha y / k \tag{2}$$

$$y = c + i + x \tag{3}$$

$$\dot{k} = i - nk \tag{4}$$

$$\dot{d} = \bar{r}d - x - nd \tag{5}$$

m denotes the maximum feasible debt-capital ratio. Let be $m < 1$. In addition let the constraint be operative $d = mk$. Now insert this into (5) and regroup $x = m\bar{r}k - mnk - m\dot{k}$. Then get rid of y, i and x in (3) by means of (1), (4) as well as $x = m\bar{r}k - mnk - m\dot{k}$ to arrive at $(1-m)\dot{k} = k^{\alpha} - c - (m\bar{r} - mn + n)k$. Let be $\bar{r} > n$.

Households maximize their utility within an infinite horizon:

$$W = \int_0^\infty \log(c) \exp(-\rho t) dt \to \max_c \qquad (6)$$

subject to

$$(1-m)\dot{k} = k^\alpha - c - (m\bar{r} - mn + n)k \qquad (7)$$

Here $\log(c)$ symbolizes the utility function, and ρ stands for the discount rate. The solution to this optimal control problem is:

$$\dot{c}/c = \frac{\alpha k^{-\beta} - m\bar{r}}{1-m} - n - \rho \qquad (8)$$

In the steady state, consumption per head remains unchanged $\dot{c} = 0$. This together with (8) produces:

$$k^\beta = \frac{\alpha}{(1-m)(n+\rho) + m\bar{r}} \qquad (9)$$

Compare this with $r = \alpha k^{-\beta}$ to get the domestic interest rate $r = (1-m)(n+\rho) + m\bar{r}$. We posit $\bar{r} < r$, since otherwise the country would not be a constrained debtor. This in turn presupposes $\bar{r} < n + \rho$. Evidently an increase in the discount rate lowers capital per head. The same is valid of an increase in the growth rate (in the foreign interest rate, respectively). But an increase in the maximum debt ratio raises capital per head. Moreover we have $d = mk$. A rise in the discount rate leads to a fall in foreign debt per head. The same holds for a rise in the growth rate (in the foreign interest rate). Naturally a rise in the maximum debt ratio causes a rise in foreign debt per head.

The next point refers to stability. The model can be enshrined in a system of two differential equations $\dot{c} = g(c, k)$ and $\dot{k} = h(c, k)$, cf. (7) and (8). A lift in k reduces $\dot{c}$, and a lift in c reduces $\dot{k}$. Now set $\dot{c} = 0$ and reshuffle:

$$k^\beta = \frac{\alpha}{(1-m)(n+\rho) + m\bar{r}} \qquad (10)$$

An increase in ρ lowers k, and an increase in m raises k. Beyond that set $\dot{k} = 0$, which implies:

$$c = k^{\alpha} - (m\bar{r} - mn + n)k \tag{11}$$

A rise in ρ has no influence on c, yet a rise in m falls on c. Figure 17 contains the phase diagram. As an outcome, the steady state is a saddle point.

For the rest of this section we discuss the process of adjustment. Let us begin with an increase in the discount rate. At the start the economy is in the steady state. Capital per head and foreign debt per head stay put. Then the discount rate goes up. As a response, the $\dot{c} = 0$ line shifts to the left, see figure 18. In the short run, the shock pushes up consumption per head and pulls down investment per head. In the medium run, capital per head declines, and so does income per head. That is why consumption per head shrinks, too. By virtue of d = mk, foreign debt per head comes down. Ultimately the economy approximates to a new steady state. Capital per head and foreign debt per head do no longer vary. Consumption per head settles down at a lower level. The streamline illuminates the dynamics.

Further regard an increase in the maximum debt ratio. Initially the economy is in the long-run equilibrium. Capital per head and foreign debt per head are uniform. In the phase diagram, the steady state lies in point 0, cf. figure 19. Now the constraint becomes relaxed. The $\dot{c} = 0$ line shifts to the right, and the $\dot{k} = 0$ line is displaced downwards. In the short run, the shock gives rise to an upward jump in both foreign debt per head and capital per head that does not affect assets per head (see point 1). In the medium run, capital per head and foreign debt per head dwindle. Therefore consumption per head deteriorates. In due course the economy reaches a new long-run equilibrium. Capital per head and foreign debt per head do not stir any more. The terminal value of consumption per head is situated below its initial value (point 2).

Contemplate a numerical example with $\alpha = 0.2$, $\rho = 0.05$, n = 0.03 and $\bar{r} = 0.06$. In the steady state with m = 0, we have k = 3.1436, d = 0, c = 1.1631 and r $= n + \rho = 0.08$. It applies $n < \bar{r} < r$. Now let the maximum debt ratio rise to 0.1. In the short run, this brings up capital per head k = 3.4929 and foreign debt per head d = 0.3493. In the new steady state, however, capital per head k = 3.2447 and consumption per head c = 1.1583 are less than before.

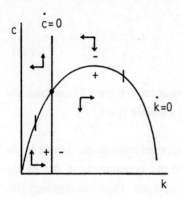

Figure 17
Phase Diagram

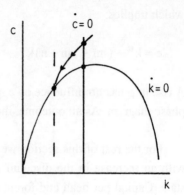

Figure 18
Increase in Discount Rate

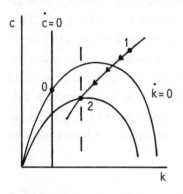

Figure 19
Increase in Maximum Debt Ratio

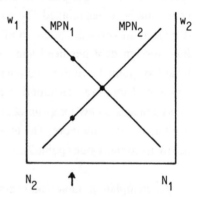

Figure 1 (Chap. IV)
Introducing Labour Mobility

CHAPTER IV. LABOUR MOBILITY

1. Introducing Labour Mobility

1.1. Model

International growth increasingly involves labour migration. Labour moves to the country which offers the highest wages. This development is especially true of single markets such as the European Union, which are based on free trade and unhampered factor movements. The investigation will be carried out within a Solow model comprising two countries where capital is perfectly mobile. Let technology be identical across countries $Y_i = K_i^\alpha N_i^\beta$ with $\alpha > 0$, $\beta > 0$ and $\alpha + \beta$ = 1. Firms maximize profits under perfect competition. For that reason, the interest rate in country i is governed by the marginal product of capital in country i $r_i = \partial Y_i / \partial K_i$. Likewise the wage rate in a country is governed by its marginal product of labour $w_i = \partial Y_i / \partial N_i$. Perfect capital mobility leads to the equalization of interest rates $r_1 = r_2$. Therefore the marginal products of capital coincide $\partial Y_1 / \partial K_1 = \partial Y_2 / \partial K_2$. Analogously perfect labour mobility causes wage rates to be equalized $w_1 = w_2$. Thus the marginal products of labour agree, too, $\partial Y_1 / \partial N_1 = \partial Y_2 / \partial N_2$.

So far the model is composed of six equations:

$$Y_i = K_i^\alpha N_i^\beta \tag{1}$$

$$r = \alpha Y_i / K_i \tag{2}$$

$$w = \beta Y_i / N_i \tag{3}$$

From this one can conclude:

$$\frac{Y_1}{Y_2} = \frac{K_1}{K_2} = \frac{N_1}{N_2} \tag{4}$$

Broadly speaking, equation (4) can be interpreted in either of two ways, cf. also chapter II, particularly section 4. First, if there were no labour mobility, then the given allocation of labour would determine the allocation of capital and output. Second, since by assumption labour mobility does exist, the allocation of labour, capital and output is indeterminate. This result, however, seems to be inconsistent with empirical evidence. To overcome this difficulty, we postulate a third, immobile factor, say land (climate, natural resources).

Consider again a production function of the Cobb-Douglas type $Y_i = K_i^\alpha N_i^\beta Z_i^\gamma$, exhibiting constant returns to scale $\alpha > 0$, $\beta > 0$, $\gamma > 0$ and $\alpha + \beta + \gamma = 1$. Here Z_i denotes land. Firms once more maximize profits under perfect competition. Hence a country's interest rate corresponds to its marginal product of capital $r_i = \partial Y_i / \partial K_i$. Similarly the wage rate matches the marginal product of labour $w_i = \partial Y_i / \partial N_i$. At this stage, the model is made up of six equations:

$$Y_i = K_i^\alpha N_i^\beta Z_i^\gamma \tag{5}$$

$$r = \alpha Y_i / K_i \tag{6}$$

$$w = \beta Y_i / N_i \tag{7}$$

These equations yield:

$$\frac{Y_1}{Y_2} = \frac{K_1}{K_2} = \frac{N_1}{N_2} = \frac{Z_1}{Z_2} \tag{8}$$

So the given allocation of land determines the allocation of labour, capital and output.

Figure 1 (see p. 138) illustrates the basic idea of introducing labour mobility. MPN_i symbolizes the marginal product of labour in country i, which is a declining function of labour input, respectively. At first suppose that there is no labour mobility. In the diagram, this is marked by an arrow. In the case depicted there, the marginal product of labour in country 1 exceeds that of country 2. As a consequence, the wage rate of country 1 surpasses that of country 2. Then introduce labour mobility. As a reaction, labour moves from country 2 to country 1, thereby lowering the wage rate in country 1 and raising the wage rate in country 2, until the wage rates are equalized. What will be the implications for international economic growth?

At this point, two cases will be distinguished. Either land is constant, or it grows at the natural rate. To begin with, have a look at the case that land is constant. The production function can be expressed in terms of growth rates $\hat{Y} = \alpha\hat{K} + \beta\hat{N} + \gamma\hat{Z}$. Let labour grow at the natural rate $\hat{N} = n$. Land is constant $\hat{Z} = 0$. In the steady state, output expands at the same rate as capital $\hat{Y} = \hat{K}$. This provides $\hat{Y} = \beta n / (\beta + \gamma)$. That is to say, income per head falls, which is inconvenient from the point of view of modelling. Now, instead, regard the case that land grows at the natural rate $\hat{Z} = n$. This furnishes $\hat{Y} = n$. That means, income per head is uniform, which appears to be better suited. Henceforth we shall start from the premise that technical progress is land-augmenting at the natural rate $\hat{Z} = n$. It is worth noting that this choice has no unfavourable side effects.

In the current section, we shall proceed in two steps. As a point of departure, we shall study an economy without labour mobility. Then, against this background, we shall inaugurate labour mobility. To begin with, we assume that there is no labour mobility. More precisely, we consider two countries with capital mobility but without labour mobility.

The model consists of eleven equations:

$$Y_i = K_i^{\alpha} N_i^{\beta} Z_i^{\gamma} \tag{9}$$

$$r = \alpha Y_i / K_i \tag{10}$$

$$\dot{F}_i + \dot{K}_i = s(Y_i + rF_i) \tag{11}$$

$$\dot{N}_i = nN_i \tag{12}$$

$$\dot{Z}_i = nZ_i \tag{13}$$

$$F_1 = -F_2 \tag{14}$$

In equation (11) we admit equal saving rates across countries $s_1 = s_2 = s$, and in equation (12) we posit equal rates of labour growth $n_1 = n_2 = n$. Here α, β, γ, n, s, F_i, K_i, N_i and Z_i are exogenous, while r, $\dot{F}_i$, $\dot{K}_i$, $\dot{N}_i$, Y_i and $\dot{Z}_i$ are endogenous. There are as many equations as variables.

The model will now be recast in per capita terms:

$$y_i = k_i^{\alpha} z_i^{\gamma} \tag{15}$$

$$r = \alpha y_i / k_i \tag{16}$$

$$\dot{f}_i + \dot{k}_i = s(y_i + rf_i) - nf_i - nk_i \tag{17}$$

$$f_1 = -cf_2 \tag{18}$$

z_i stands for land per head, and c is the international allocation of labour c = N_2/N_1. In this instance α, γ, c, f_i, k_i, n, s and z_i are given, whereas $\dot{f}_i$, $\dot{k}_i$, r and y_i adjust themselves.

In the steady state, capital per head and foreign assets per head grind to a halt. Therefore the steady state can be represented by a system of seven equations:

$$y_i = k_i^{\alpha} z_i^{\gamma} \tag{19}$$

$$r = \alpha y_i / k_i \tag{20}$$

$$nf_i + nk_i = s(y_i + rf_i) \tag{21}$$

$$f_1 = -cf_2 \tag{22}$$

At this stage α, γ, c, n, s and z_i are fixed, while f_i, k_i, r and y_i are flexible.

What are the distinguishing qualities of the steady state? From (19) and (20) follows $k_1 = zk_2$ and $y_1 = zy_2$ with z defined as $z = (z_1/z_2)^{\gamma/(\beta+\gamma)}$. Take the sum over (21), observing $f_1 = -cf_2$, $k_1 = zk_2$ and $y_1 = zy_2$, to get $nk_i = sy_i$. This together with (21) proves that the foreign positions must be balanced:

$$f_i = 0 \tag{23}$$

From $nk_i = sy_i$ and $y_i = k_i^{\alpha} z_i^{\gamma}$ one can extract:

$$k_i^{\beta+\gamma} = \frac{sz_i^{\gamma}}{n} \tag{24}$$

$$y_i^{(\beta+\gamma)/\alpha} = \frac{sz_i^{\gamma}}{n} \tag{25}$$

$$c_i = (1-s)y_i \tag{26}$$

(26) states consumption per head, given that no foreign assets are held. Over and above that, without losing generality, let land per head of country 1 be greater than that of country 2. Then, as an outcome, capital per head of country 1 goes beyond that of country 2. And the same applies to output per head as well as to consumption per head ($y_1 > y_2$, $c_1 > c_2$).

At this juncture we shall install labour mobility. Taking the same avenue as before, the model can be written down as a system of thirteen equations:

$$Y_i = K_i^\alpha N_i^\beta Z_i^\gamma \tag{27}$$

$$r = \alpha Y_i / K_i \tag{28}$$

$$w = \beta Y_i / N_i \tag{29}$$

$$\dot{F}_i + \dot{K}_i = s(Y_i + rF_i) \tag{30}$$

$$\dot{N}_i = nN_i \tag{31}$$

$$\dot{Z}_i = nZ_i \tag{32}$$

$$F_1 = -F_2 \tag{33}$$

Here α, β, γ, n, s, F_i, K_i, N_i and Z_i are exogenous, whereas r, w, $\dot{F}_i$, $\dot{K}_i$, $\dot{N}_i$, Y_i and $\dot{Z}_i$ are endogenous. The number of equations exceeds the number of variables by one.

From (27), (28) and (29) one can derive $Y_1/Y_2 = K_1/K_2 = N_1/N_2 = Z_1/Z_2$. In per capita terms, this can be reformulated as $y_1 = y_2$, $k_1 = k_2$ and $z_1 = z_2$. In other words, the countries agree in output per head, capital per head and land per head. Further take the difference of (30) $(\dot{f}_1 + \dot{k}_1) - (\dot{f}_2 + \dot{k}_2)$, noting $f_1 = -cf_2$, $k_1 = k_2$ as well as $y_1 = y_2$, which provides $\dot{f}_1 = srf_1 - nf_1$ and $\dot{k}_1 = sy_1 - nk_1$. After what has been said, the model simplifies to a system of five equations:

$$y_1 = k_1^\alpha z_1^\gamma \tag{34}$$

$$r = \alpha y_1 / k_1 \tag{35}$$

$$w = \beta y_1 \tag{36}$$

$$\dot{f}_1 = srf_1 - nf_1 \tag{37}$$

$$\dot{k}_1 = sy_1 - nk_1 \tag{38}$$

In these circumstances $\dot{f}_1$, $\dot{k}_1$, r, w and y_1 adjust themselves. There are as many equations as variables.

In the steady state, the stock variables per head cease to adjust. Accordingly the steady state can be described by a system of five equations:

$$y_1 = k_1^\alpha z_1^\gamma \tag{39}$$

$$r = \alpha y_1 / k_1 \tag{40}$$

$$w = \beta y_1 \tag{41}$$

$$f_1 = 0 \tag{42}$$

$$nk_1 = sy_1 \tag{43}$$

Here f_1, k_1, r, w and y_1 are flexible.

What are the key characteristics of the steady state? (42) has it that the foreign positions will again be balanced. From (39) and (43) together with z redefined as $z = z_1 = z_2$ one can infer:

$$k_1^{\beta+\gamma} = \frac{sz^\gamma}{n} \tag{44}$$

In addition $c_i = (1-s)y_i$ implies $c_1 = c_2$. Put differently, consumption per head is equal in both countries. To summarize, owing to the high degree of symmetry, the countries are identical in per capita terms. With respect to stability, the model can be compressed to a system of two differential equations $\dot{f}_1 = g_1(f_1, k_1)$ and $\dot{k}_1 = h_1(f_1, k_1)$. In the same way as in chapter II, the steady state turns out to be stable.

1.2. Numerical Example

To elucidate the preceding section, take a numerical example. First we shall calculate the steady state without labour mobility. Second we shall try to find out the steady state with labour mobility. And third we shall keep track of the process of adjustment. The parameters of the model are $\alpha = 0.2$, $\beta = 0.7$, $\gamma = 0.1$, $n = 0.03$ and $s = 0.1$. Let land in period 0 be $Z(0) = 100$, $Z_1(0) = 50$ and $Z_2(0) = 50$. Put another way, the area of the countries is the same size.

1) Steady state without labour mobility. Let labour in period 0 be $N(0) = 100$, $N_1(0) = 40$ and $N_2(0) = 60$. For the result see table 20. On this basis, table 21 indicates the country shares. The area of country 1 is 50% of world area. The labour of country 1 is 40% of world labour. As an upshot, the capital of country 1 is 41% of world capital. The output of country 1 is 41% of world output. And the consumption of country 1 is 41% of world consumption.

2) Steady state with labour mobility. Let labour in period 0 be $N(0) = 100$. This implies $N_1(0) = N_2(0) = 50$. For the result see table 20, period ∞. Correspondingly, table 22 points out the country shares. The labour of country 1 is 50% of world labour. The capital of country 1 is 50% of world capital etc.

The comparative evaluation of the steady states yields, cf. table 20: Labour mobility reduces land per head of country 1 and increases land per head of country 2. It lowers capital per head of country 1 and raises capital per head of country 2. The same is true of output per head. However, labour mobility leaves no impact on the foreign positions. It deteriorates consumption per head in country 1 and improves consumption per head in country 2. More exactly, consumption per head in country 1 drops by 2.8%, while consumption per head in country 2 climbs by 2.3%. Labour mobility brings up consumption per head at world level c by 0.2%. The underlying reason is that the reallocation of labour enhances world income per head, world savings per head and world capital per head.

Table 20

Process of Adjustment (Introducing Labour Mobility)

	0	0'	∞
z_1	1.2500	1	1
z_2	0.8333	1	1
k_1	4.6314	4.4941	4.5040
k_2	4.4025	4.4941	4.5040
k	4.4941	4.4941	4.5040
y_1	1.3894	1.3506	1.3512
y_2	1.3208	1.3506	1.3512
y	1.3482	1.3506	1.3512
f_1	0	- 0.7890	0
f_2	0	0.7890	0
c_1	1.2505	1.1729	1.2161
c_2	1.1887	1.2582	1.2161
c	1.2134	1.2156	1.2161

Table 21

Country Shares without Labour Mobility

	1	2
Z	50	50
N	40	60
K	41	59
Y	41	59
C	41	59

Table 22

Country Shares with Labour Mobility

	1	2
Z	50	50
N	50	50
K	50	50
Y	50	50
C	50	50

3) Process of adjustment. Initially the economy is in the steady state without labour mobility, see table 23, period 0. Then labour mobility is introduced. For the instantaneous effects see table 23, period 0'. Labour moves from country 2 to country 1. Put differently, labour migrates from the high-density country to the low-density country. Likewise capital flows from country 2 to country 1. That is why country 1 becomes a debtor, and country 2 a creditor. We assume here that migrants do not own wealth since they are young. Consumption in country 1 goes up, whereas consumption in country 2 comes down. For the instantaneous effects in per capita terms, see table 20, period 0'. Capital per head of country 1 falls, even though capital of country 1 rises. Similarly consumption per head of country 1 worsens, while consumption per head of country 2 becomes better, as does consumption per head at world level.

Figure 2 shows the time paths of capital per head. Figure 3 visualizes the foreign positions. In the long-run equilibrium before shock, the foreign position of country 1 is balanced. In the short run, country 1 becomes a debtor. In the intermediate run, foreign debt per head of country 1 declines. And in the long-run equilibrium after shock, the foreign position of country 1 is again balanced. Figu-

148

res 4 and 5 graph consumption per head. The natives of country 2 win, yet the natives of country 1 lose. What is more, the overall gain exceeds the overall loss.

Table 23
Instantaneous Effects of Introducing Labour Mobility

	0	0'
Z_1	50	50
Z_2	50	50
N_1	40	50
N_2	60	50
K_1	185.26	224.71
K_2	264.15	224.71
K	449.41	449.41
Y_1	55.576	67.531
Y_2	79.248	67.531
Y	134.82	135.06
F_1	0	- 39.45
F_2	0	39.45
C_1	50.018	58.644
C_2	71.323	62.912
C	121.34	121.56

149

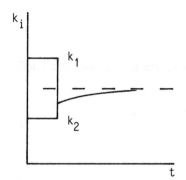

Figure 2
Capital Per Head

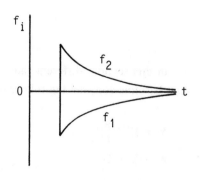

Figure 3
Foreign Assets Per Head

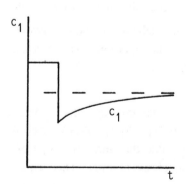

Figure 4
Consumption Per Head
in Country 1

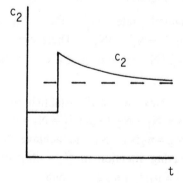

Figure 5
Consumption Per Head
in Country 2

2. Different Rates of Labour Growth

In this section, different rates of labour growth will be sketched out briefly. As a baseline consider the following model:

$$Y_i = K_i^\alpha N_i^\beta Z_i^\gamma \tag{1}$$

$$r = \alpha Y_i / K_i \tag{2}$$

$$w = \beta Y_i / N_i \tag{3}$$

This provides $Y_1/Y_2 = K_1/K_2 = N_1/N_2 = Z_1/Z_2$. That means, the allocation of labour, capital and output depends on the given allocation of land, which is identical to what has been said above.

Let labour reproduce at the constant rate n_i, which differs across countries. In the fertile country, labour supply increases rather rapidly, causing the wage rate to decline. Hence labour moves to the other country until wage rates balance again. Assume that birth and death rates change in the process of migration, due to cultural adjustment. The change in labour supply is based on reproduction and outmigration $\dot{N}_i^s = n_i N_i - N_{ij}$. Labour demand, on the other hand, grows at the natural rate $\dot{N}_i^d = nN_i$. Equilibrium in the labour market involves $n_i N_i - N_{ij} = nN_i$. Therefore the rate of outmigration is constant $N_{ij}/N_i = n_i - n$. And if $n_i > n$, then $N_{ij}/N_i > 0$.

Next we shall establish the natural rate n. Take the time derivative of $N = N_1 + N_2$ to get $\dot{N} = \dot{N}_1 + \dot{N}_2$. Moreover insert $\dot{N}_1 = n_1 N_1 - N_{12}$ as well as $\dot{N}_2 = n_2 N_2 + N_{12}$ to achieve $\dot{N} = n_1 N_1 + n_2 N_2$. Put this into $\dot{N} = \dot{N}_1 + \dot{N}_2$, paying attention to $\dot{N}_1 = nN_1$ and $\dot{N}_2 = nN_2$, to check $\dot{N} = nN$. Then equate $\dot{N} = n_1 N_1 + n_2 N_2$ and $\dot{N} = nN$ to reach the natural rate $n = n_1 N_1 / N + n_2 N_2 / N$. Define $z_i = Z_i / Z$, which is somewhat different from what has been said before. This furnishes $N_i / N = z_i$. Finally we obtain:

$$n = z_1 n_1 + z_2 n_2 \tag{4}$$

In other words, weighting the national reproduction rates by the international allocation of land gives the world reproduction rate.

Assembling all component parts, the model can be captured by a system of thirteen equations:

$$Y_i = K_i^\alpha N_i^\beta Z_i^\gamma \tag{5}$$

$$r = \alpha Y_i / K_i \tag{6}$$

$$w = \beta Y_i / N_i \tag{7}$$

$$\dot{F}_i + \dot{K}_i = s(Y_i + rF_i) \tag{8}$$

$$\dot{N}_i = nN_i \tag{9}$$

$$\dot{Z}_i = nZ_i \tag{10}$$

$$F_1 = -F_2 \tag{11}$$

As it stands, this harmonizes with the model built in the preceding section.

In the steady state, as a result, capital per head and output per head are uniform $k_1 = k_2$, $y_1 = y_2$. The foreign positions will be balanced $f_1 = f_2 = 0$. And consumption per head coincides among countries $c_1 = c_2$. Further an increase in the reproduction rate of country 1 raises the natural rate n, thereby lowering consumption per head in both countries.

CHAPTER V. FIXED WAGE RATE

1. Closed Economy

As a point of reference take a closed economy. Let us begin with a Solow model. At first assume a flexible wage rate. The model can be characterized by a system of four equations:

$$Y = K^\alpha N^\beta \tag{1}$$

$$w = \beta Y / N \tag{2}$$

$$\dot{K} = sY \tag{3}$$

$$\dot{N} = nN \tag{4}$$

Here α, β, n, s, K and N are exogenous, while w, $\dot{K}$, $\dot{N}$ and Y are endogenous. The equilibrium wage rate amounts to $w^* = \beta(s/n)^{\alpha/\beta}$. Of course there is always full employment.

Now, instead, assume a fixed wage rate. More exactly, let the wage rate exceed its equilibrium value $w > w^*$. As a consequence, the economy will suffer from unemployment. But what will be the implications of unemployment for the process of economic growth? The model can be represented by a system of four equations:

$$Y = K^\alpha L^\beta \tag{5}$$

$$w = \beta Y / L \tag{6}$$

$$\dot{K} = sY \tag{7}$$

$$\dot{N} = nN \tag{8}$$

Here L denotes labour demand and N labour supply. In this case α, β, n, s, w, K and N are given, whereas $\dot{K}$, L, $\dot{N}$ and Y adjust themselves.

The growth rate of capital can be defined as $\hat{K} = \dot{K} / K$. This together with $\dot{K} = sY$ yields $\hat{K} = sY / K$. Further combine $Y = K^\alpha L^\beta$ and $w = \beta Y / L$ to ascertain:

$$Y = K(\beta / w)^{\beta / \alpha} \tag{9}$$

Obviously an increase in the wage rate reduces labour demand and thus output. To illustrate this, consider a numerical example with $\alpha = 0.2$. There a 1% rise in the wage rate lowers labour demand by 5% and output by 4%. In addition, from $\hat{K} = sY / K$ and (9) one can infer:

$$\hat{K} = s(\beta / w)^{\beta / \alpha} \tag{10}$$

As a result, this is the growth rate of the stock of capital. A lift in the wage rate depresses the growth rate of capital. Yet a lift in the saving rate enhances the growth rate. In the numerical example, a 1% rise in the wage rate cuts back the growth rate by 4%. And a 1% rise in the saving rate brings up the growth rate by 1%.

Besides from (9) one can deduce $\hat{Y} = \hat{K}$, and $w = \beta Y / L$ implies $\hat{Y} = \hat{L}$. Putting these pieces together, we find:

$$\hat{Y} = \hat{K} = \hat{L} = s(\beta / w)^{\beta / \alpha} \tag{11}$$

That is to say, output, capital and labour demand expand at the same constant rate. Beyond that, an increase in the wage rate slows down the process of expansion. Conversely, an increase in the saving rate speeds up this process. Last but not least we have:

$$\hat{Y} = \hat{K} = \hat{L} < n \tag{12}$$

In other words, the growth rate of output, capital and labour demand falls short of the natural rate (i.e. the growth rate of labour supply).

Next have a look at the process of adjustment induced by an increase in the wage rate. Initially let the economy be in the steady state with full employment. Output, capital, labour demand and labour supply grow at the same rate. Then the wage rate goes up. In the short run, firms lay off workers, so unemployment comes into existence. This lowers output, income, savings, investment and hence capital formation. In the medium run, the growth rate of capital declines. This in turn diminishes the growth rates of labour demand and output. Therefore output, capital and labour demand expand more slowly than labour supply. This means, inter alia, that the rate of unemployment rises period by period. Over and above that, the new steady state is identical to the medium-run equilibrium.

Figures 1 until 4 show the time paths of the main variables, where figures 1 until 3 are drawn on a semilogarithmic scale. Figure 1 depicts the autonomous path of labour supply and the induced path of labour demand. At the beginning, labour demand grows at the same rate as labour supply, clearing the labour market. Then abruptly the shock reduces labour demand, which from this time on grows at a lower rate. The time path of capital becomes flatter but does not drop suddenly (figure 2). And the movement of output reminds one of that of labour demand (figure 3).

Finally we address an overlapping generations model with a fixed wage rate. The model consists of three equations:

$$Y = K^{\alpha} L^{\beta} \tag{13}$$

$$w = \beta Y / L \tag{14}$$

$$K_{+1} = \beta \delta Y \tag{15}$$

Here α, β, δ, w and K are exogenous, while K_{+1}, L and Y are endogenous. The growth rate of capital is $\hat{K} = (K_{+1} - K)/K$. Substitute $K_{+1} = \beta \delta Y$ to get $\hat{K} = \beta \delta Y / K - 1$. Along the same lines as before, $Y = K(\beta / w)^{\beta/\alpha}$ can be derived. Insert this into $\hat{K} = \beta \delta Y / K - 1$ to verify:

$$\hat{K} = \beta \delta (\beta / w)^{\beta/\alpha} - 1 \tag{16}$$

An increase in the wage rate pulls down the growth rate. The other way round, an increase in the saving rate pushes up the growth rate. This underlines the importance of the results obtained in the Solow model.

156

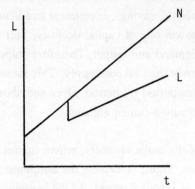

Figure 1
Demand and Supply of Labour

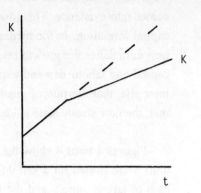

Figure 2
Stock of Capital

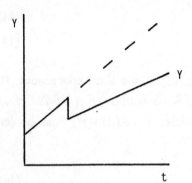

Figure 3
Output (Income)

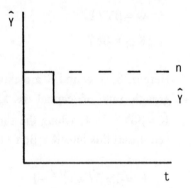

Figure 4
Growth Rate of Output

2. Perfect Capital Mobility

In this section, we shall make use of the factor price frontier. As a baseline regard a closed economy with a flexible wage rate. The model is composed of three equations:

$$y = k^\alpha \tag{1}$$

$$r = \alpha y / k \tag{2}$$

$$w = \beta y \tag{3}$$

Here α, β and k are exogenous, while r, w and y are endogenous.

From this follows $r = \alpha k^{-\beta}$ and $w = \beta k^\alpha$. Now dispense with k to realize:

$$w = \beta(\alpha / r)^{\alpha/\beta} \tag{4}$$

This is the equation of the factor price frontier FPF, see figure 5. It reveals all feasible combinations of interest rate and wage rate. Moreover a few words will be said on factor intensity. Eliminate y in (1) and (2) to check:

$$w = \beta r k / \alpha \tag{5}$$

This is the equation of the factor intensity ray k, cf. figure 5. Its slope $\beta k/\alpha$ hinges on the capital-labour ratio k. In the closed economy with a flexible wage rate, the capital intensity is given, whereas factor prices adjust themselves. In figure 5, this is marked by the point of intersection. An increase in capital intensity raises the wage rate and lowers the interest rate.

Second contemplate a small open economy with perfect capital mobility and a flexible wage rate. In these circumstances, the interest rate becomes exogenous, while capital intensity and the wage rate are endogenous, see figure 6. An increase in the foreign interest rate depresses capital intensity and the domestic wage rate.

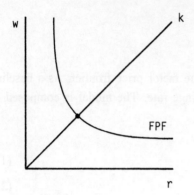

Figure 5
Closed Economy,
Flexible Wage Rate

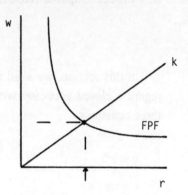

Figure 6
Perfect Capital Mobility,
Flexible Wage Rate

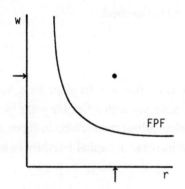

Figure 7
Perfect Capital Mobility,
Fixed Wage Rate

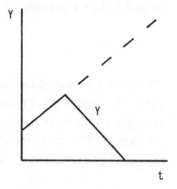

Figure 8
Perfect Capital Mobility,
Increase in Wage Rate

Third imagine a small open economy with perfect capital mobility but a fixed wage rate. In this case, factor prices are given, whereas factor intensity adjusts itself. In figure 7, the foreign interest rate and the domestic wage rate are fixed at high levels. On the one hand we have $k = (\alpha / r)^{1/\beta}$, on the other hand we get $k = (w / \beta)^{1/\alpha}$. However, these two capital intensities will be equal only by chance. This has some far-reaching consequences. There exists no production yielding zero profits or positive profits. Put another way, firms are bound to make losses. Ultimately the economy must break down.

Next we shall trace out the dynamic effects of an increase in the wage rate. Originally the economy is in the steady state with full employment. Output, capital, labour demand and labour supply grow at the same rate. Against this background, the wage rate is driven up. In the short run, firms dismiss workers, so unemployment emerges. Because of this, the marginal product of capital falls short of the interest rate, hence firms must reduce capital input. On this account, the marginal product of labour becomes less than the wage rate, thus firms must cut back labour input. The economy enters a vicious circle of capital flight and unemployment. Rapidly this process brings both capital and labour input down to zero. Figure 8 plots the ensuing time path of output.

3. Imperfect Capital Mobility

In this section, we shall restrict capital mobility. The analysis will be implemented within an overlapping generations model of a small open economy featuring a fixed wage rate. m denotes again the maximum feasible debt-capital ratio (maximum debt ratio). Let be $m < 1$. In addition, let the constraint be operative $D = mK$. Domestic capital can be financed from two sources, domestic assets and foreign debt $K_{+1} = \beta \delta Y + D_{+1}$. Pay heed to $D = mK$ to verify $(1 - m)K_{+1} = \beta \delta Y$.

The complete model is made up of four equations:

$$Y = K^{\alpha} L^{\beta} \qquad (1)$$

$$w = \beta Y / L \tag{2}$$

$$(1-m)K_{+1} = \beta \delta Y \tag{3}$$

$$N_{+1} = (1+n)N \tag{4}$$

In this setting α, β, δ, m, n, w, K and N are given, whereas K_{+1}, L, N_{+1} and Y adjust themselves.

The growth rate of capital can be defined as $\hat{K} = (K_{+1} - K) / K$. Observe (3) and rearrange $\hat{K} = \beta \delta Y / (1-m)K - 1$. For the same reasons as above it holds $Y = K(\beta / w)^{\beta/\alpha}$. Join this together to arrive at:

$$\hat{K} = \frac{\beta \delta}{1-m} \left(\frac{\beta}{w} \right)^{\beta/\alpha} - 1 \tag{5}$$

Evidently, an increase in the wage rate lowers the growth rate of capital. An increase in the saving rate raises the growth rate. And the same is true of an increase in the maximum debt ratio. More generally the findings can be expressed as:

$$\hat{D} = \hat{Y} = \hat{K} = \hat{L} = \frac{\beta \delta}{1-m} \left(\frac{\beta}{w} \right)^{\beta/\alpha} - 1 < n \tag{6}$$

Further $D = mK$ and $Y = K(\beta / w)^{\beta/\alpha}$ combine to give:

$$D / Y = m(w / \beta)^{\beta/\alpha} \tag{7}$$

A rise in the wage rate enhances the debt-income ratio. And the same applies to a rise in the maximum debt ratio. The time pattern of output is identical to that exhibited for the closed economy, cf. figure 3.

4. Land as Immobile Factor

In this section we come back to a small open economy with perfect capital mobility and a fixed wage rate. Once more the factor price frontier will take a prominent place. The underlying model can be caught by a system of four equations:

$$Y = K^{\alpha} L^{\beta} Z^{\gamma} \qquad (1)$$

$$r = \alpha Y / K \qquad (2)$$

$$w = \beta Y / L \qquad (3)$$

$$p = \gamma Y / Z \qquad (4)$$

Equation (4) states that the land rent p corresponds to the marginal product of land. Here α, β, γ, r, w and Z are exogenous, while p, K, L and Y are endogenous.

From equations (1) up to (4) one can conclude $Y = (\alpha Y / r)^{\alpha}$ $(\beta Y / w)^{\beta} (\gamma Y / p)^{\gamma}$, which furnishes:

$$1 = \left(\frac{\alpha}{r}\right)^{\alpha} \left(\frac{\beta}{w}\right)^{\beta} \left(\frac{\gamma}{p}\right)^{\gamma} \qquad (5)$$

This is the equation of the factor price frontier, see figure 9. The foreign interest rate and the domestic wage rate determine the domestic land rent. A lift in the interest rate cuts back the land rent, as does a lift in the wage rate. Consider a numerical example with $\alpha = 0.2$, $\beta = 0.7$ and $\gamma = 0.1$. There a 1% increase in the wage rate reduces the land rent by 7%. Likewise a 1% increase in the interest rate reduces the land rent by 2%. Within this framework, firms do not make losses, as opposed to an economy without land.

We proceed now to a full Solow model, which rests on five equations:

$$Y = K^{\alpha} L^{\beta} Z^{\gamma} \qquad (6)$$

$$r = \alpha Y / K \tag{7}$$

$$w = \beta Y / L \tag{8}$$

$$\dot{F} + \dot{K} = s(Y + rF) \tag{9}$$

$$\dot{N} = nN \tag{10}$$

In this instance α, β, γ, n, r, s, w, F, K, N and Z are fixed, whereas $\dot{F}$, $\dot{K}$, L, $\dot{N}$ and Y are flexible.

Equations (6) until (8) yield:

$$Y^{\gamma} = \left(\frac{\alpha}{r}\right)^{\alpha} \left(\frac{\beta}{w}\right)^{\beta} Z^{\gamma} \tag{11}$$

Judging from this, a rise in the wage rate lowers labour demand, capital input and thus output. In the numerical example, a 1% increase in the wage rate reduces labour demand by 8%, capital input by 7% and output by 7% as well. Similarly a rise in the interest rate leads to a fall in capital input, labour demand and output.

Next we tackle dynamics. The production function can be transformed in terms of growth rates $\hat{Y} = \alpha\hat{K} + \beta\hat{L} + \gamma\hat{Z}$. Owing to $r = \alpha Y/K$, we have $\hat{K} = \hat{Y}$. And due to $w = \beta Y/L$, we get $\hat{L} = \hat{Y}$. Moreover we postulate that land cannot be augmented $\hat{Z} = 0$. Of course this differs from the assumptions made so far. Assembling all component parts, we achieve:

$$\hat{Y} = \hat{K} = \hat{L} = 0 \tag{12}$$

As a consequence, output, capital input and labour demand are invariant.

Besides substitute $\dot{K} = 0$ into (9) and solve for $\hat{F}$:

$$\hat{F} = sY / F + rs \tag{13}$$

First of all, the growth rate of foreign assets is positive. A lift in the wage rate cuts back output and thereby the growth rate of foreign assets. A lift in the saving rate drives up the growth rate. And a lift in foreign assets brings down the growth rate of foreign assets. Asymptotically the growth rate converges to:

$$\hat{F} = rs \qquad\qquad (14)$$

A boost in the interest rate speeds up the growth of foreign assets. From $C = (1-s)(Y + rF)$, in the same way, one can extract the growth rate of consumption $\hat{C} = rs$.

Coming to an end, we shed some light on the process of adjustment generated by an increase in the wage rate. At the beginning the economy is in the steady state with full employment. Labour supply and labour demand expand at the natural rate $\hat{L} = \hat{N} = n$. Capital, output and foreign assets expand at a somewhat lower rate $\hat{F} = \hat{Y} = \hat{K} = \beta n / (\beta + \gamma)$. Then, at once, the wage rate moves up. In the short run, firms lay off workers, so unemployment occurs. This goes along with a decline in both capital input und output. The fall in capital input, in turn, is accompanied by a rise in foreign assets. Strictly speaking, these changes may be equal in amount. In the medium run, however, labour demand, capital input and output are constant, round by round. Labour supply, on the other hand, continues to grow at the natural rate. That is why the unemployment rate becomes larger period by period. Beyond that savings contribute to the accumulation of foreign assets. But subsequently the growth of foreign assets slows down. As time passes away, the economy tends to a new steady state. Labour demand, capital input and output are still uniform. And foreign assets expand at the small rate $\hat{F} = rs$.

Figures 10 till 13 visualize the time paths of the chief variables, being drawn on a semilogarithmic scale. Figure 10 contains the exogenous path of labour supply and the endogenous path of labour demand. At the start, labour demand grows at the same rate as labour supply, the market clears. Then the shock diminishes labour demand, which henceforth stays at the lower level. The time paths of capital input and output are isomorphic to that of labour demand, see figures 11 and 12. In a stylized way, figure 13 graphs how foreign assets travel through time. At the outset, foreign assets grow at a high rate. Then the shock pushes up foreign assets, yet in future they expand at a lower rate.

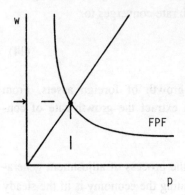

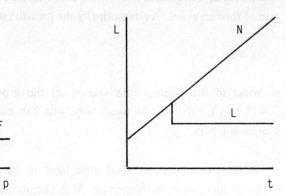

Figure 9
Fixed Wage Rate,
Flexible Land Rent

Figure 10
Demand and Supply of Labour

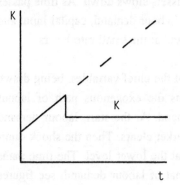

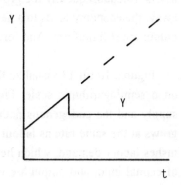

Figure 11
Stock of Capital

Figure 12
Output

Eventually overlapping generations will be sketched out briefly. $F_{+1} = \beta\delta Y - K$ implies $\hat{F} = 0$, so foreign assets do not change in the long run. This is in remarkable contrast to the conclusions drawn in the Solow model.

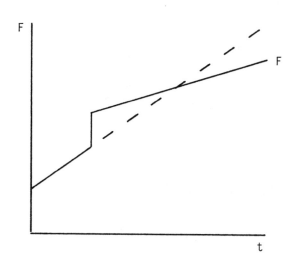

Figure 13
Foreign Assets

CHAPTER VI. ENDOGENOUS GROWTH

1. Closed Economy

This chapter deals with endogenous growth, putting special emphasis on the AK model. As a point of departure, in section 1, we shall take a closed economy. Then, in section 2, we shall proceed to a small open economy. Capital mobility will be either perfect or imperfect. And the country in question will be either a debtor or a ceditor. In section 3, we shall inquire into a two-country model. And finally, in section 4, we shall study an infinite horizon model.

Let us begin with a closed economy. Firms produce a homogeneous commodity by making use of physical and human capital. The production function is $Y = AK$, where K denotes aggregate capital, Y output and A productivity (A = const). Raw labour, i.e. labour without human capital, is unproductive. That is why it does not enter the production function. Households save a certain fraction of income $S = sY$ with s = const. Savings are invested $I = S$. Investment in turn adds to the stock of capital $\dot{K} = I$. From this follows $\dot{K} = sY$. The model can be characterized by a system of two equations:

$$Y = AK \tag{1}$$
$$\dot{K} = sY \tag{2}$$

Here s, A and K are exogenous, while $\dot{K}$ and Y are endogenous.

Equations (1) and (2) yield:

$$\hat{Y} = \hat{K} = sA \tag{3}$$

That means, capital and output grow at the same invariant rate. An increase in the saving rate raises the growth rate of capital and output. And the same holds for an increase in productivity. The interest rate is governed by productivity $r = A$. Substitute this into $Y = AK$ to get $Y = rK$. In other words, income consists solely

of capital income. The wage rate, i.e. the factor price of raw labour, amounts to w
= 0. The reason for this is that raw labour is unproductive.

Now it is helpful to restate the problem in per capita terms, i.e. per head of
raw labour. Let raw labour grow at a uniform rate $\dot{N} = nN$. The production
function can be written as $y = Ak$, where $k = K/N$ symbolizes capital per head
and $y = Y/N$ output per head. From $\hat{k} = \hat{K} - \hat{N}$, $\hat{y} = \hat{Y} - \hat{N}$, $\hat{Y} = \hat{K} = sA$ and
$\hat{N} = n$ one can derive:

$$\hat{y} = \hat{k} = sA - n \tag{4}$$

Put another way, capital per head and output per head expand at the same uniform rate. Equation (4) gives rise to two cases. If $sA > n$, then $\hat{y} > 0$, so output
per head grows period by period. Conversely, if $sA < n$, then $\hat{y} < 0$, so output per
head declines round by round. What is more, an increase in the saving rate brings
up the growth rate of output per head. And the same is true of an increase in productivity. However, an increase in the growth rate of raw labour cuts back the
growth rate of output per head. At this point it is important to keep in mind that
an increase in the growth rate of raw labour does not affect the growth rate of
output as such, cf. equation (3).

2. Small Open Economy

At first have a look at perfect capital mobility. The domestic production
function is $Y = AK$. The foreign interest rate r is given exogenously. Accordingly
two cases can occur. If productivity exceeds the foreign interest rate $A > r$, there
will be an extremely large capital inflow, hence the stock of capital will explode.
On the other hand, if productivity falls short of the foreign interest rate, there will
be an extremely large capital outflow, hence the country runs out of capital. This
seems to be grossly unrealistic.

Therefore we henceforth assume imperfect capital mobility. Let productivity be greater than the foreign interest rate, so the country in question will be a debtor. Domestic residents pay the interest rate r on foreign debt D, so the interest outflow totals rD. The income of domestic residents equals factor income minus interest outflow $Y - rD$. Domestic residents save a fixed proportion of their income $S = s(Y - rD)$ with s = const. Domestic investment can be financed out of two sources, domestic savings and foreign borrowing $I = S + B$. Investment in turn augments the stock of capital $\dot{K} = I$. Likewise foreign borrowing augments foreign debt $\dot{D} = B$. All of this provides $\dot{K} = s(Y - rD) + \dot{D}$. m stands for the maximum feasible debt-capital ratio (maximum debt ratio). We posit m < 1. Of course the constraint is always binding $D = mK$. Insert this into $\dot{K} = s(Y - rD) + \dot{D}$ to accomplish $(1 - m)\dot{K} = s(Y - mrK)$.

On these grounds, the model can be represented by a system of two equations:

$$Y = AK \tag{1}$$
$$(1 - m)\dot{K} = s(Y - mrK) \tag{2}$$

Here m, r, s, A and K are exogenous, whereas $\dot{K}$ and Y are endogenous.

From (1) and (2) one can conclude:

$$\hat{K} = \frac{sA - mrs}{1 - m} \tag{3}$$

As a result, this is the growth rate of capital. A > r implies A > mr, thus the growth rate is strictly positive. A rise in the saving rate proportionately enhances the growth rate of capital. A rise in productivity enhances the growth rate, too. The other way round, a rise in the foreign interest rate depresses the growth rate. Yet a rise in the maximum debt ratio enhances the growth rate. Over and above that, the small open economy expands more rapidly than the closed economy. Besides, by virtue of $Y = AK$, we have $\hat{Y} = \hat{K}$. Thanks to $D = mK$, we find $\hat{D} = \hat{K}$. And on account of $C = (1 - s)(Y - mrK)$, we get $\hat{C} = \hat{K}$.

170

To illustrate this, consider a numerical example. At first regard an economy without capital mobility. Suppose A = 0.2 and s = 0.1. In this situation, the growth rate is $\hat{K} = 0.02$. Instead contemplate an economy with capital mobility. Let be m = 0.1 and r = 0.1. In these circumstances, the growth rate is higher than before $\hat{K} = 0.0211$. To assess this, take an initial stock of capital of 100. How much will this be after a period of 100 years? Granted an annual growth rate of 2% the stock of capital expands from 100 to 739. But granted an annual growth rate of 2.11%, the stock of capital expands from 100 to 825. The message is that small differences in growth rates lead to large differences in levels. Further a lift in the saving rate from 0.1 to 0.2 pushes up the growth rate from 0.0211 to 0.0422, that is proportionately. A lift in productivity from 0.2 to 0.4 drives up the growth rate from 0.0211 to 0.0433, that is more than proportionately. A cut in the foreign interest rate from 0.1 to 0.05 brings up the growth rate from 0.0211 to 0.0216, that is far less than proportionately. And a lift in the maximum debt ratio from 0.1 to 0.2 elevates the growth rate from 0.0211 to 0.0225.

Next we shall be concerned with the processes of adjustment kicked off by diverse shocks. First imagine an increase in the saving rate. At the beginning, the economy is in the steady state. The stock of capital expands at a constant rate. Then the saving rate goes up. Instantaneously this raises savings and thus the growth rate of capital. With this, the economy is in the new steady state. The stock of capital expands again at a constant rate which, however, lies well above the initial rate. Figure 1 shows the kinked time path of the stock of capital on a semilogarithmic scale. Figure 2 visualizes the associated path of consumption. On the one hand, there is a one-time reduction in consumption. After that, on the other hand, consumption expands at a higher speed.

Second catch a glimpse of an increase in productivity. Originally the economy is in the permanent equilibrium. The stock of capital expands at a uniform rate. Then productivity rises. At once this augments income, savings and the growth rate of capital. With this, the economy has jumped into the new permanent equilibrium. The stock of capital expands at a uniform rate which is higher than the pre-shock rate. Figure 3 portrays the dynamics of output. The disturbance has two effects, as can easily be seen. There is a sudden increase in output, and from that time on output grows faster. Analogously figure 4 plots the dynamics of consumption.

171

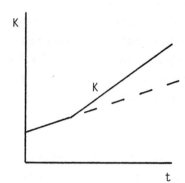

Figure 1
Increase in Saving Rate

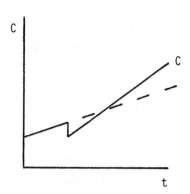

Figure 2
Increase in Saving Rate

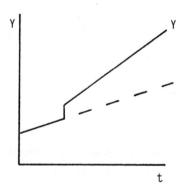

Figure 3
Rise in Productivity

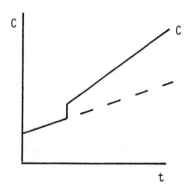

Figure 4
Rise in Productivity

Third take a glance at an increase in the foreign interest rate. At the start, capital accumulates at an invariant rate. Then the foreign interest rate is bid up. Instantaneously the interest outflow swells, which curbs the income of domestic residents. Savings drop, and so does the growth rate of capital. After that capital accumulates once more at an invariant rate which, however, lies well below the initial rate. Figure 5 depicts the transition of the stock of capital. And figure 6 graphs the pattern of consumption. There is a one-time cut in consumption and, even worse, a fall in the growth rate.

Fourth introduce capital mobility. At the outset, let the economy be in a steady state without capital mobility. The stock of capital expands at the constant rate $\hat{K} = sA$. Then capital mobility is allowed. At once there will be a huge capital inflow. This builds up the stock of capital and output. Properly speaking, foreign debt rises by the same amount as the stock of capital. The income of domestic residents $Y - rD$ becomes larger, since $A > r$. This in turn enhances savings and the growth rate of capital. With this the economy enters the new steady state. The stock of capital expands again at a constant rate which is greater than the initial rate. Figure 7 exhibits the time path of the stock of capital. The shock lifts capital and, even better, its growth rate. Figure 8 reveals the accompanying path of consumption.

So far we assumed that productivity exceeds the foreign interest rate $A > r$. Now we shall suppose the reverse case $A < r$. As a consequence, the country in question will be a creditor. What does imperfect capital mobility signify in this context? Obviously there is a high risk in lending abroad, so lenders impose a constraint. More precisely, the foreign assets of a country must not go beyond a critical level, expressed in terms of its capital stock (maximum feasible foreign asset ratio).

Domestic residents earn the interest rate r on foreign assets F, hence the interest inflow totals rF. The income of domestic residents consists of capital income and the interest inflow $Y + rF$. Households save a certain fraction of their income $S = s(Y + rF)$ with s = const. Savings can be used for two purposes, investment and foreign lending $I + E = S$. Investment in turn contributes to the accumulation of capital $\dot{K} = I$. And foreign lending contributes to the accumulation of foreign assets $\dot{F} = E$. Putting together these building blocks we gain $\dot{K} = s(Y + rF) - \dot{F}$. m denotes here the maximum foreign asset ratio. Naturally the

173

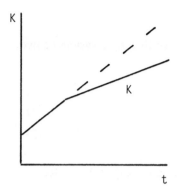

Figure 5
Increase in Foreign Interest Rate

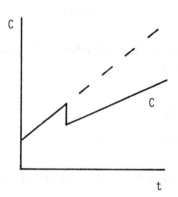

Figure 6
Increase in Foreign Interest Rate

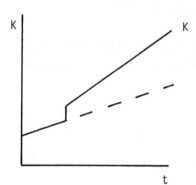

Figure 7
Introducing Capital Mobility

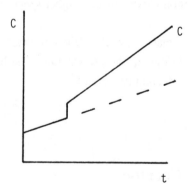

Figure 8
Introducing Capital Mobility

constraint will always be operative $F = mK$. Combine this with $\dot{K} = s(Y + rF) - \dot{F}$ to reach $(1+m)\dot{K} = s(Y + mrK)$.

Having laid this groundwork, the model can be described by a system of two equations:

$$Y = AK \tag{4}$$

$$(1+m)\dot{K} = s(Y + mrK) \tag{5}$$

In this instance m, r, s, A and K are given, whereas $\dot{K}$ and Y adjust themselves.

Equations (4) and (5) produce:

$$\hat{K} = \frac{sA + mrs}{1 + m} \tag{6}$$

An increase in the saving rate raises the growth rate of capital, and the same holds for an increase in productivity. This confirms the results obtained for the debtor country. An increase in the foreign interest rate raises the growth rate, too, as opposed to the conclusions drawn for the debtor country. The same is valid for an increase in the maximum foreign asset ratio. Over and above that, the small open economy expands at a higher speed than the closed economy.

In summary, in each of the countries, whether high-tech or low-tech, capital mobility brings up the growth rate. The high-tech country will be a debtor, and the low-tech country a creditor.

3. Two Countries

The investigation will be carried out within an AK model featuring different technologies but equal saving rates. The production function is $Y_i = A_i K_i$. The interest rate earned on domestic capital equals productivity $r_i = A_i$. By way of contrast, r symbolizes the interest rate paid on foreign debt. Let the productivity of country 1 be greater than the productivity of country 2 $A_1 > A_2$. Then the interest rate paid on foreign debt will be situated somewhere in between $r_1 > r > r_2$. Accordingly country 1 will raise loans in country 2. Generally speaking, the high-productive country will be a debtor, and the low-productive country a creditor. The foreign assets of country 2 must not surpass a critical level, expressed in terms of its capital stock. m stands again for the maximum foreign asset ratio. Of course the constraint will be binding $F_2 = mK_2$.

Pursuing the same approach as before, the model can be captured by a system of six equations:

$$Y_1 = A_1K_1 \tag{1}$$
$$Y_2 = A_2K_2 \tag{2}$$
$$\dot{K}_1 = s(Y_1 - rD_1) + \dot{D}_1 \tag{3}$$
$$\dot{K}_2 = s(Y_2 + rF_2) - \dot{F}_2 \tag{4}$$
$$F_2 = mK_2 \tag{5}$$
$$D_1 = F_2 \tag{6}$$

Equations (2), (4) and (5) provide:

$$\hat{K}_2 = \frac{sA_2 + mrs}{1 + m} \tag{7}$$

As a corollary, we have $\hat{K}_2 > sA_2$. That means, capital mobility increases the growth rate of country 2. Further equations (1), (3), (5) and (6) deliver $\hat{K}_1 = sA_1 - mK_2(rs - \hat{K}_2)/K_1$. Eliminate $\hat{K}_2$ by means of (7) to arrive at:

$$\hat{K}_1 = sA_1 - \frac{msK_2}{K_1} \frac{r - A_2}{1 + m} \tag{8}$$

We find $\hat{K}_1 < sA_1$, which comes somewhat as a surprise. That is to say, capital mobility reduces the growth rate of country 1. Instantaneously, to be fair, capital mobility increases the stock of capital in country 1. For the time pattern see the

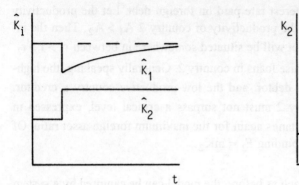

Figure 9
Introducing Capital Mobility

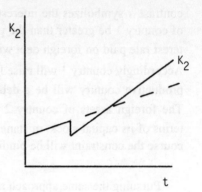

Figure 10
Capital in Country 2

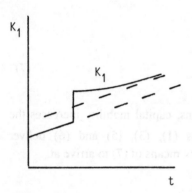

Figure 11
Capital in Country 1

following figures. In addition we postulate $\hat{K}_1 > \hat{K}_2$, because otherwise there would be a switch in regime (i.e. the foreign debt of country 1 must not exceed a critical level, expressed in terms of its capital stock). Then, as time goes to infinity, the growth rate of country 1 tends to sA_1, which indeed is its initial value, cf. figure 9. Incidentally a few remarks will be made with respect to consumption. Owing to $C_2 = (1-s)(Y_2 + mrK_2)$, we get $\hat{C}_2 = \hat{K}_2$. And due to $C_1 = (1-s)(Y_1 - mrK_2)$, we find that $\hat{C}_1$ approximates to sA_1.

Finally we shall trace out the process of adjustment set in motion by introducing capital mobility. At the beginning, let the world be in a steady state without capital mobility. Both growth rates are invariant, where the growth rate of country 1 is bigger than the growth rate of country 2. Then we inaugurate capital mobility. At once there will be a large capital flow from country 2 to country 1, restricted only by the maximum foreign asset ratio of country 2. This in turn depresses the growth rate of country 1 and enhances the growth rate of country 2. Put differently, there is a tendency towards equalization in growth rates. In the medium run, the growth rate of country 2 is uniform. And the growth rate of country 1 recovers step by step, in the long run coming back to its initial value.

Figures 10 till 13 display the time paths on a semilogarithmic scale. First have a look at capital in country 2, the reader may wish to consult figure 10. In the state of financial autarky, capital expands at a constant rate. Then the opening of financial markets has two distinct effects. On the one hand it diminishes the stock of capital. On the other hand it augments the growth rate of capital. Next consider capital in country 1, cf. figure 11. The shock lifts capital, but cuts its growth rate. With the lapse of time, the growth rate becomes restored. In the end, the economy expands at the initial rate, yet at a higher level. Besides regard consumption in country 2, see figure 12. Capital mobility improves both consumption and its growth rate. At last take consumption in country 1, cf. figure 13. The time structure is reminiscent of that of capital.

Summary: In the short run, capital mobility increases world output, world income, world consumption, world savings and world investment. And in the long run, it raises the world growth rate.

178

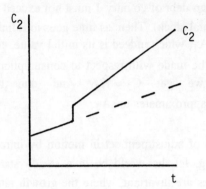

Figure 12
Consumption in Country 2

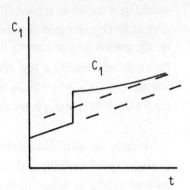

Figure 13
Consumption in Country 1

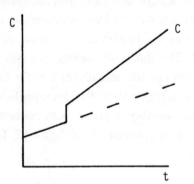

Figure 14
Optimal Growth Rate

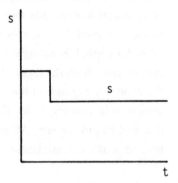

Figure 15
Optimal Saving Rate

4. Infinite Horizon

In the preceding sections, we assumed a fixed saving rate. In the current section, instead, we shall suppose intertemporal optimization within an infinite horizon. The small open economy with imperfect capital mobility serves as a framework. Let technology be of the AK type. In addition let productivity be greater than the foreign interest rate $A > r$, so the country will be a debtor.

It applies $\dot{K} = Y - rD - C + \dot{D}$, where $Y - rD$ is the income of domestic residents and $Y - rD - C$ are their savings. m denotes the maximum debt ratio. We posit $m < 1$. From $\dot{K} = Y - rD - C + \dot{D}$ together with $D = mK$ and $Y = AK$ follows $\dot{K} = (AK - mrK - C)/(1-m)$. Households maximize utility within an infinite horizon:

$$W = \int_0^\infty \log(C)\exp(-\rho t)dt \to \max_C \tag{1}$$

subject to

$$\dot{K} = \frac{AK - mrK - C}{1 - m} \tag{2}$$

Here $\log(C)$ symbolizes the utility function, and ρ the discount rate.

The solution to this problem is:

$$\hat{C} = \frac{A - mr}{1 - m} - \rho \tag{3}$$

As a result, this is the optimal growth rate. For the method see Barro and Sala-i-Martin (1995). First of all, the growth rate is invariant. An increase in the discount rate lowers the growth rate. An increase in productivity raises the growth rate. An increase in the foreign interest rate lowers the growth rate. And an increase in the maximum debt ratio raises the growth rate. If the discount rate be-

180

comes very large, then the growth rate becomes negative. What is more, capital and output expand at the same rate as consumption $\hat{Y} = \hat{K} = \hat{C}$.

Now we shall derive the optimal saving rate. To begin with, reformulate (2) as $\hat{K} = (A - mr - C/K)/(1 - m)$. Then compare this with (3), which produces $C = \rho K/(1 - m)$. Further substitute $D = mK$ and $Y = AK$ into $C = (1 - s)(Y - rD)$ to find out $C = (1 - s)(AK - mrK)$. Finally confront this with $C = \rho K/(1 - m)$ and solve for s:

$$s = 1 - \frac{\rho}{(1 - m)(A - mr)} \tag{4}$$

This is the optimal saving rate. Above all the saving rate is uniform. A rise in the discount rate reduces the saving rate. A rise in productivity increases the saving rate. A rise in the foreign interest rate reduces the saving rate. And the same is true of a rise in the maximum debt ratio.

To conclude, we shall keep track of the process of adjustment set in motion by inaugurating capital mobility. At the start let the economy be in the steady state without capital mobility. Consumption expands at the constant rate $\hat{C} = A - \rho$. Then capital mobility is allowed. Instantaneously, as a reaction, there will be a large capital inflow. This in turn builds up the stock of capital and output. The addition to capital goes along with an addition to foreign debt of equal size $\Delta D = \Delta K$. The income of domestic residents $Y - rD$ increases, since $A > r$. The optimal saving rate, however, declines. These two effects push up consumption $C = (1 - s)(Y - rD)$. And the rise in savings leads to a rise in the growth rates of capital and consumption. With this, the economy is already in the new steady state. Consumption expands at a constant rate which lies well above the initial rate. Figure 14 shows the time path of consumption, drawn on a semilogarithmic scale. Capital mobility at once lifts consumption. After that consumption expands at a higher rate. Figure 15 illustrates the response of the saving rate.

Conclusion

First of all have a look at a small open economy with perfect capital mobility (chapter I). For the small open economy, the foreign interest rate is given exogenously. And under perfect capital mobility, the domestic interest rate agrees with the foreign interest rate. Take for instance a Solow model featuring the dynamics of foreign assets. The income of domestic residents is composed of factor income and the interest inflow. Domestic residents save a fixed proportion of their income. The current account surplus is the sum of net exports and the interest inflow. The current account surplus in turn contributes to the accumulation of foreign assets. As a rule, the steady state will be stable. As an exception, however, if the rate of labour growth is very low, then the steady state will be unstable. And the same holds when the foreign interest rate (the saving rate, respectively) is very high.

What are the chief properties of the steady state? An increase in the saving rate does affect neither capital per head nor output per head. But it brings up foreign assets per head. And it improves consumption per head, provided the foreign interest rate exceeds the rate of labour growth. An increase in the rate of labour growth leaves no impact on capital per head and output per head either. Yet it reduces both foreign assets per head and consumption per head. An increase in the foreign interest rate cuts back both capital per head and output per head. On the other hand, it drives up foreign assets per head. If the foreign interest rate is low, the shock depresses consumption per head. Conversely, it the foreign interest rate is high, the shock enhances consumption per head. All of this is in remarkable contrast to the results obtained for the closed economy.

The high-saving country makes loans abroad. It holds foreign assets and earns interest on them. The interest inflow allows the country to finance net imports of commodities. The interest inflow gives rise to a current account surplus and a trade deficit. The last point requires that the foreign interest rate is greater than the growth rate, which generally will be assumed. The other way round, the low-saving country raises loans abroad. It pays interest on foreign debt. In order to finance the interest outflow, the country must be a net exporter of commodities. The interest outflow gives rise to a current account deficit and a trade surplus.

The high-saving country will be a creditor, the low-saving country a debtor. The fast-growing country will be a debtor, the slow-growing country a creditor. If the foreign interest rate is high, the country will be a creditor. If the foreign interest rate is low, the country will be a debtor.

Now we shall trace out the processes of adjustment induced by two alternative shocks, an increase in the saving rate and an increase in the foreign interest rate. Let us begin with an increase in the saving rate. Initially the economy is in the steady state. The current account surplus per head and foreign assets per head are constant. Investment per head, capital per head and output per head do not move. And the same applies to consumption per head and net imports per head. Against this background, the saving rate goes up. In the short run, this deteriorates consumption per head. Net imports per head fall, so the current account surplus per head rises. Investment per head does not respond.

In the medium run, owing to the rise in the current account surplus per head, foreign assets per head accumulate. Capital per head and output per head remain unchanged, since investment per head did not respond. Due to the growth of foreign assets per head, the interest inflow per head swells. This in turn augments the per-capita income of domestic residents, hence consumption per head recovers. That is why net imports per head come up, too. And the swell of the interest inflow per head lifts the current account surplus per head. Here a comment is in place with respect to the underlying export function. The part of domestic output that is neither consumed nor invested at home, will be exported. And what about the import function? The part of domestic consumption and investment, that is not produced at home, will be imported.

As time proceeds, the economy appoaches a new steady state. The current account surplus per head and foreign assets per head are again constant. Investment per head, capital per head and output per head do not move. And the same is true of consumption per head and net imports per head. Taking the sum over the process of adjustment as a whole, the current account surplus per head and foreign assets per head went up. Investment per head, capital per head and output per head did not change. Consumption per head and net imports per head rose.

Second regard the dynamic consequences of an increase in the foreign interest rate. At the start the economy is in the long-run equilibrium. The current account surplus per head and foreign assets per head are uniform. Investment per head, capital per head and output per head do not vary. And the same is valid of consumption per head as well as of net imports per head. In these circumstances, the foreign interest rate is bid up.Therefore, instantaneously, capital flows out, thus adjusting the marginal product of capital. Capital per head drops, while foreign assets per head jump up.

In the intermediate run, foreign assets per head continue to pile up. Capital per head and output per head, on the other hand, stay put, being pegged by the foreign interest rate. Consumption per head, net imports per head and the current account surplus per head do climb. Asymptotically the economy converges to a new long-run equilibrium. The current account surplus per head and foreign assets per head are once more uniform. Investment per head, capital per head and output per head do not vary. And the same is valid of consumption per head as well as of net imports per head. Over the process as a whole, the current account surplus per head and foreign assets per head mounted. Conversely investment per head, capital per head and output per head descended. Consumption per head became better or worse, and net imports per head grew.

So far we assumed an instantaneous adjustment of the capital stock. Now, instead, we shall suppose a delayed adjustment. This can be attributed to the presence of installation costs. Properly speaking, investment serves to fill the gap between the desired and the actual stock of capital step by step.

Next we shall keep track of the transitional dynamics generated by an increase in the foreign interest rate. Originally the economy is in the steady state. Foreign assets per head and capital per head do not move. Then, abruptly, the foreign interest rate goes up. In the short run, this raises the interest inflow per head and thereby the current account surplus per head. In addition, the shock lowers desired capital per head and investment per head. In the intermediate run, the rise in the current account surplus per head leads to the growth of foreign assets per head. And the fall in investment per head causes a decline in capital per head. With the lapse of time, the economy reaches a new steady state. The motion of foreign assets per head and capital per head grinds to a halt.

At this point we leave the Solow model and come to the overlapping generations model. The steady state proves to be stable. The other characteristics of the steady state are also rather similar. For example, contemplate an increase in patience, which is the counterpart of the saving rate. Then, with a one-period delay, foreign assets per head jump from the old steady state up to the new one.

Finally we proceed to the infinite horizon model and shed some light on the process of adjustment released by a one-time increase in labour. At the beginning, the economy is in the permanent equilibrium. Foreign assets per head and capital per head are constant. Then, all of a sudden, labour augments, thus diminishing both foreign assets per head and capital per head. Instantaneously, there will be a large capital inflow. For that reason, capital per head recovers, whereas foreign assets per head decline a second time. More exactly, the recovery of capital per head is equal in amount to the decline of foreign assets per head. In the short-run equilibrium after shock, capital per head is back at its original level, but foreign assets per head are severely lowered. With this the economy has entered the new permanent equilibrium. In summary we get a one-time reduction in foreign assets per head as well as in consumption per head.

Chapter II deals with two large countries, given again perfect capital mobility. This means that interest rates are equalized among countries. In section 1, the focus is on different saving rates. We posit overlapping generations with identical technologies and equal rates of labour growth. The steady state turns out to be stable.

We address now the distinguishing qualities of the steady state. The high-saving country will be a creditor. It runs a current account surplus and a trade deficit. Conversely, the low-saving country will be a debtor. It runs a current account deficit and a trade surplus. Let country 1 be a creditor and country 2 a debtor. Then a rise in the saving rate of country 1 pushes up capital per head and output per head in each of the countries. The shock raises foreign assets per head of country 1 and foreign debt per head of country 2. As a rule, consumption per head improves in each of the countries, in the first line in country 1. This clearly differs from the conclusions drawn for the small open economy.

Further catch a glimpse of the transitional dynamics kicked off by an increase in the saving rate of country 1. Let country 1 be a creditor and country 2 a debtor. Initially the economy is in the steady state. In country 1, the current account surplus per head and foreign assets per head do not stir. The same holds for the current account deficit per head and the foreign debt per head of country 2. In each of the countries, investment per head and capital per head are invariant. In this situation the saving rate of country 1 goes up. In the short run, both the current account surplus per head of country 1 and the current account deficit per head of country 2 climb. Analogously, in each of the countries, investment per head shoots up.

In the medium run, in country 1, the rise in the current account surplus per head contributes to the accumulation of foreign assets per head. In country 2, the rise in the current account deficit per head makes foreign debt per head grow round by round. In each of the countries, the rise in investment per head boosts capital per head. In due course the economy reaches a new steady state. In country 1, the current account surplus per head and foreign assets per head do not move any longer. The same applies to the current account deficit per head and the foreign debt per head of country 2. In each of the countries, investment per head and capital per head are invariant. Taking the sum over the process, foreign assets per head of country 1 and foreign debt per head of country 2 went up, as did capital per head in each of the countries.

In section 3, we discuss technical progress abroad. The reform countries in Central Eastern Europe and the newly industrialized countries in South East Asia are going to enter the world market. How are the advanced countries affected by this? For instance, what does this imply with respect to capital flows and consumption? Imagine a world composed of two countries, the advanced country and the emerging country. Then the shock can be interpreted, in terms of the model, as a one-time technical progress abroad. The analysis is conducted within a Solow model marked by equal saving rates and equal rates of labour growth.

What are the salient features of the steady state? An increase in the efficiency of country 2 has no influence on capital per head and output per head in country 1. Yet it brings up capital per head and output per head in country 2. The foreign positions are always balanced. Consumption per head of country 1 stays put, while that of country 2 becomes better.

186

Moreover we study the dynamic consequences of a one-time technical progress abroad. At the start the economy is in the steady state. In each of the countries, the current account and the foreign position are balanced. Investment per head and capital per head are uniform, in country 1 as well as in country 2. The interest rates equilibrate, and so do the marginal products of capital. Against this background, the efficiency of country 2 increases. This enhances the marginal product of capital in country 2 and hence its interest rate. Therefore, instantaneously, capital flows from country 1 to country 2. In other words, capital per head of country 1 drops, and capital per head of country 2 springs up. This elevates the marginal product of capital in country 1 and depresses that of country 2 until they are equalized. Obviously country 1 becomes a creditor, and country 2 a debtor.

How does the short-run equilibrium look? In country 1, capital per head and output per head are lower as compared to their pre-shock values. Foreign assets per head, on the other hand, are higher than before. Strictly speaking, the addition to foreign assets per head is the same size as the subtraction from capital per head. The interest rate lies well above its initial level, as does consumption per head. In country 2, capital per head and output per head are bigger than at the start. The same is true of foreign debt per head, where the change of foreign debt per head is equal to the change of capital per head. The interest rate surpasses its original level, as does consumption per head.

In the intermediate run, both foreign assets per head of country 1 and foreign debt per head of country 2 come down again. In each of the countries, capital per head keeps on surging. As time goes on, the economy gravitates towards a new steady state. In each of the countries, the current account and the foreign position are once more balanced. In each of the countries, too, investment per head and capital per head are uniform. To sum up, in country 1, capital per head and consumption per head return to their points of departure, respectively. In country 2, however, capital per head and consumption per head settle at a higher level.

Section 4 is concerned with different rates of labour growth. The investigation is carried out within an overlapping generations model characterized by equal saving rates and identical technologies. As a finding, the steady state is stable. The fast-growing country will be a debtor, with foreign debt per head being equal to zero. The other way round, the slow-growing country will be a creditor, with foreign assets per head lying well above zero. More precisely, as time goes to infinity, the foreign debt of country 1 tends to explode, as do the foreign assets of country 2. The foreign debt per head of country 1 converges to zero, and the foreign assets per head of country 2 converge to a finite value.

To illustrate this, consider the process of adjustment set in motion by an increase in the rate of labour growth of country 1. Initially, let the economy be in a steady state with equal rates of labour growth. Accordingly the foreign positions are balanced. Against this background, the rate of labour growth of country 1 rises. In the short run, capital moves from country 2 to country 1. Country 1 becomes a debtor, and country 2 a creditor. Capital per head declines in each of the countries. In the medium run, the foreign debt per head of country 1 decumulates. But the foreign assets per head of country 2 continue to accumulate. And capital per head continues to shrink in each of the countries. As time passes away, the economy tends to a new steady state. The foreign debt per head of country 1 has been redeemed altogether, while the foreign assets per head of country 2 are strictly positive.

The leading subject of chapter III is imperfect capital mobility. Evidently there is a high risk in lending abroad as contrasted with lending at home. Above all this includes the political risk and the currency risk. Therefore lenders have an incentive to impose a constraint on lending abroad. This can be modelled in either of two ways. First, the foreign debt of a country must not exceed a critical level, expressed in terms of its capital stock as a collateral (maximum feasible debt-capital ratio). Second, the interest rate to be paid by the borrowing country to the lending country is an increasing function of the debt-capital ratio.

Section 1 rests on a Solow model of a small open economy with a fixed debt ratio. The basic idea is that an increase in the stock of capital permits the country in question to raise more loans abroad, thereby increasing its stock of capital even further. What about the steady state? An increase in the saving rate pushes up both capital per head and output per head. Foreign debt per head rises, whereas the domestic interest rate falls. An increase in the growth rate pulls down both capital per head and output per head. Foreign debt per head descends, yet the domestic interest rate mounts. An increase in the maximum debt ratio augments both capital per head and output per head. It enhances foreign debt per head and depresses the domestic interest rate. All of this is in contradistinction to the case of perfect capital mobility. There an increase in the saving rate does not impinge on capital per head and output per head. Foreign debt per head diminishes, and the domestic interest rate holds fast.

Next take a glance at the dynamic effects of an increase in the saving rate. At the beginning, the economy is in the permanent equilibrium. Capital per head and foreign debt per head are invariant. Then, spontaneously, the saving rate jumps up. In the short run, this cuts back consumption per head and lifts investment per head. In the intermediate run, thanks to the rise in investment per head, capital per head expands. And according to the maximum debt ratio, foreign debt per head is allowed to grow, too. This in turn reinforces the expansion of capital per head. As a consequence, output per head, income per head and consumption per head improve. In the end, the economy reaches a new permanent equilibrium.

Section 2 relies on an overlapping generations model of a small open economy marked by an endogenous interest rate. Properly speaking, the interest rate to be paid on foreign debt is an increasing function of the debt-capital ratio. The intuition behind this section is that an increase in the debt-capital ratio drives up the interest rate, thus reducing capital per head. What are the key attributes of the steady state? A rise in the saving rate lowers the debt-capital ratio and the interest rate, which raises capital per head. A rise in the growth rate boosts the debt-capital ratio and the interest rate, thereby putting downward pressure on capital per head. This is in sharp contrast to the results achieved under perfect capital mobility.

Section 3 is based on an infinite horizon model of a small open economy with a fixed debt ratio. First a few words will be said on the steady state. An increase in the discount rate reduces capital per head. The same applies to an increase in the growth rate (in the foreign interest rate, for that matter). And an increase in the maximum debt ratio brings up capital per head.

Next the process of adjustment will be sketched out briefly. Originally the economy is in the steady state. Capital per head and foreign debt per head do not move. Then, abruptly, the discount rate goes up. In the short run, this augments consumption per head and diminishes investment per head. In the medium run, capital per head comes down step by step. By virtue of the maximum debt ratio, foreign debt per head must be paid back to a certain extent. On these grounds, output per head, income per head and consumption per head dwindle. Ultimately the economy approximates to a new steady state.

Chapter IV is devoted to labour mobility. International growth increasingly involves labour migration: Labour moves to the country which offers the best wages. This development is especially true of single markets such as the European Union, which are based on free trade and unhampered factor movements.

Section 1 derives the effects of introducing labour mobility. The analysis is implemented within a Solow model consisting of two countries under perfect capital mobility. There are equal saving rates, equal rates of labour growth and identical technologies. Perfect labour mobility implies that wage rates are equalized, so the marginal products of labour coincide as well. If there were no labour mobility, then the given allocation of labour would determine the allocation of capital and output. Since by assumption there is labour mobility, the allocation of labour, capital and output is indeterminate. This however seems to be inconsistent with empirical evidence. To overcome this difficulty, we postulate a third, immobile factor, say land. Then the given allocation of land determines the allocation of labour, capital and output.

What is the basic idea of the model? At first suppose that there is no labour mobility. Let the marginal product of labour in country 1 exceed that in country 2. Correspondingly, the wage rate in country 1 is larger than that in country 2. Then inaugurate labour mobility. At once labour moves from country 2 to country 1. The wage rate of country 1 falls, whereas the wage rate of country 2 rises, until they are equalized. How does this affect international growth?

We inquire now into the long-run effects of installing labour mobility. We posit that labour density is low in country 1 and high in country 2, before labour mobility, respectively. Then labour mobility reduces land per head in country 1 and increases land per head in country 2. The same is valid of capital per head, output per head and consumption per head. But the foreign positions are always balanced. What is more, labour mobility improves world consumption per head. The reason for this is that the reallocation of labour raises world income per head, world savings per head and world capital per head.

Next we probe into the dynamics of introducing labour mobility. At the start let the economy be in a steady state without labour mobility. Then labour mobility becomes allowed. Instantaneously labour moves from country 2 to country 1, that is from the high-density country to the low-density country. Because of this, capital moves from country 2 to country 1, too. Hence country 1 becomes a debtor, and country 2 a creditor. In this connection, we assume that migrants do not own wealth, since they are young. Consumption in country 1 goes up, and consumption in country 2 comes down. What does this mean in per capita terms? Capital per head in country 1 drops, even though capital itself springs up there. Consumption per head in country 1 deteriorates, while consumption per head in country 2 improves, as does consumption per head at world level.

How do the foreign positions develop? In the long-run equilibrium before shock, the foreign position of country 1 is balanced. In the short run, country 1 becomes a debtor. In the medium run, foreign debt per head of country 1 decreases. And in the long-run equilibrium after shock, the foreign position of country 1 is again balanced. Last but not least, with respect to consumption per head, the natives of country 2 win, whereas the natives of country 1 lose. Beyond that, the overall gain surpasses the overall loss.

Section 2 treats the case of different rates of labour growth. Apart from this we take the same avenue as before. Particularly, the given allocation of land determines the allocation of labour, capital and output. Let labour reproduce at a constant rate which differs across countries. In the "fertile" country, labour supply increases rather rapidly, causing the wage rate to decline. Thus labour moves to the other country until the wage rates balance again. Besides assume that birth and death rates change in the process of migration. Then, as a consequence, weighting the national reproduction rates by the international allocation of land gives the world reproduction rate. In the steady state, capital per head, output per head and consumption per head are equalized among countries. The foreign positions are always balanced. An increase in the rate of labour growth of country 1 drives up the rate of labour growth of country 2, thereby cutting back consumption per head in each of the countries.

In chapter V we postulate a fixed wage rate. As a point of reference, in section 1, consider a closed economy. Let the wage rate exceed its equilibrium level, so there will be unemployment. How does this impinge on economic growth? At first have a look at the steady state. An increase in the wage rate lowers the growth rate of output, capital and labour demand. Conversely an increase in the saving rate raises the growth rate of output, capital and labour demand.

Next we keep track of the process of adjustment induced by an increase in the wage rate. At the beginning let the economy be in a steady state with full employment. Output, capital and labour demand grow at the natural rate. Against this background, the wage rate goes up. In the short run, the shock reduces labour demand, so unemployment arises. This in turn leads to a cut in output, income, savings, investment and hence in capital formation. In the medium run, therefore, the expansion of capital, labour demand and output slows down. More precisely, the common growth rate of output, capital and labour demand falls short of the natural rate. Particularly labour demand develops at a lower speed than labour supply, which drives up the rate of unemployment step by step. Besides the new steady state is identical to the medium-run equilibrium.

In section 2, we address a small open economy under perfect capital mobility. Suppose that the foreign interest rate and the domestic wage rate are fixed at high levels. Then, as a consequence, there is no production yielding zero or positive profits. Put another way, firms are bound to make losses. Ultimately the economy must break down.

Now catch a glimpse of transitional dynamics. Initially let the economy be in a permanent equilibrium with full employment. Output, capital and labour demand grow at the same rate as labour supply. In this situation, there is a hike in the wage rate. In the short run, the shock depresses labour demand, so unemployment occurs. The marginal product of capital falls well below the interest rate, hence firms decrease capital input. That is why the marginal product of labour falls well below the wage rate, thus firms dismiss even more workers. The economy enters a vicious circle of capital flight and unemployment. Rapidly this process squeezes both capital and labour input down to zero.

In section 3, we proceed to a small open economy under imperfect capital mobility, assuming a fixed debt ratio. What are the salient features of the steady state? An increase in the wage rate pulls down the growth rate of capital. An increase in the saving rate pushes up the growth rate of capital. And the same applies to an increase in the maximum debt ratio.

192

In section 4, we introduce land as an immobile factor. The analysis is conducted within a small open economy under perfect capital mobility. According to the factor price frontier, an increase in the wage rate brings about a decline in the land rent. Firms suffer no losses, as opposed to the case of an economy without land. The major properties of the steady state are: A rise in the wage rate slows down the expansion of foreign assets and consumption. A rise in the saving rate speeds up the expansion of foreign assets and consumption. The same holds for a rise in the foreign interest rate.

Moreover we trace out the process of adjustment. Originally the economy is in a long-run equilibrium marked by full employment. Then the wage rate moves up. In the short run, the shock restricts labour demand, so unemployment comes into existence. This in turn lowers capital input and output. The fall in capital input is associated with a rise in foreign assets. Here cause and effect may well be the same size. In the intermediate run, labour demand, capital input and output are constant. Labour supply, on the other hand, continues to grow at the natural rate. For that reason, the rate of unemployment mounts period by period. Owing to the fact that savings are positive, foreign assets pile up. The speed of expansion of foreign assets, however, declines successively. As time goes on, the economy approaches a new long-run equilibrium. Labour demand, capital input and output are still invariant. The growth rate of foreign assets does not drop any more.

Chapter VI is concerned with endogenous growth. The AK model serves as a framework. Firms produce a homogeneous commodity by making use of physical and human capital. Raw labour (i.e. labour without human capital) is unproductive. On that ground it does not enter the production function. As a base of comparison, in section 1, we regard a closed economy. The growth rates of capital and output prove to be uniform. An increase in the saving rate lifts the growth rates of capital and output. The same is true of an increase in productivity.

In section 2, we proceed to a small open economy. Let us begin with perfect capital mobility. If productivity surpasses the foreign interest rate, there will be an extremely large capital inflow, so the stock of capital tends to explode. The other way round, if productivity stays below the foreign interest rate, there will be an extremely large capital outflow, hence the country in question will run out of capital. This, however, seems to be grossly unrealistic.

Therefore we assume imperfect capital mobility. First let productivity be higher than the foreign interest rate, thus the country will be a debtor. Here imperfect capital mobility means a fixed debt ratio. As a finding, the growth rate of capital is constant. An increase in the saving rate enhances the growth rate. The same applies to an increase in productivity. An increase in the foreign interest rate depresses the growth rate. And an increase in the maximum debt ratio elevates the growth rate. That is to say, the small open economy grows faster than the closed economy.

Second let productivity be lower than the foreign interest rate, so the country will be a creditor. What does imperfect capital mobility mean in this instance? There is a high risk in lending abroad, hence lenders impose a constraint on it. The foreign assets of a country must not exceed a critical level, expressed in terms of its capital stock (maximum feasible foreign asset ratio). As a result, a rise in the saving rate pushes up the growth rate of capital. The same is valid of a rise in productivity. This confirms the conclusions drawn for the debtor country. A rise in the foreign interest rate, too, brings up the growth rate. The same holds for an increase in the maximum foreign asset ratio. This clearly differs from the results obtained for the debtor country. Once more, the small open economy expands more rapidly than the closed economy.

To sum up, in both countries, whether high-tech or low-tech, capital mobility raises the speed of expansion. The high-tech country will be a debtor, and the low-tech country a creditor.

In section 3, we study two countries linked by imperfect capital mobility. As a setting, take an AK model with different technologies but equal saving rates. Let the productivity of country 1 be greater than that of country 2. As a consequence, country 1 will be a debtor, and country 2 a creditor. The foreign assets of country 2 must not go beyond a critical value, expressed in terms of its capital stock.

Now take a glance at the dynamic effects of introducing capital mobility. At the start, let the economy be in a steady state without capital mobility. In each of

194

the countries, the growth rate is invariant. Strictly speaking, the growth rate of country 1 exceeds that of country 2. Then capital mobility becomes inaugurated. Instantaneously, there is a large capital flow from country 2 to country 1, limited only by the maximum foreign asset ratio of country 2. This in turn reduces the growth rate of country 1 and increases that of country 2. Thus there is a tendency towards equalization in growth rates. In the medium run, the growth rate of country 2 is uniform. Yet the growth rate of country 1 recovers round by round. Asymptotically, the growth rate of country 1 converges to its initial value. Résumé: In the short run, capital mobility improves world consumption. And in the long run, capital mobility boosts the world growth rate.

Last but not least, in section 4, we suppose intertemporal optimization within an inifinite horizon. The investigation is performed within a small open economy subject to imperfect capital mobility. Let productivity surpass the foreign interest rate, hence the country will be a debtor. As an outcome, both the saving rate and the growth rate of consumption are invariant. An increase in the discount rate lowers the saving rate as well as the growth rate of consumption. An increase in productivity raises the saving rate and the growth rate of consumption. An increase in the foreign interest rate cuts back the saving rate and the growth rate of consumption. An increase in the maximum debt ratio diminishes the saving rate. In spite of that, it augments the growth rate of consumption.

Result

Let us begin with a small open economy. What are the comparative statics? An increase in the saving rate does not affect either capital per head or output per head. However, the shock raises foreign assets per head. Consumption per head improves, as long as the foreign interest rate exceeds the growth rate. An increase in the growth rate leaves no impact on capital per head and output per head. It lowers foreign assets per head and deteriorates consumption per head. An increase in the foreign interest rate reduces both capital per head and output per head. On the other hand, it pushes up foreign assets per head. As long as the foreign interest rate stays below a critical level, consumption per head becomes worse. But as soon as the foreign interest surpasses the critical level, consumption per head becomes better. All of this is in remarkable contrast to the findings for the closed economy.

The high-saving country makes loans abroad. It holds foreign assets and earns interest on them. The interest inflow allows the country to finance net imports of commodities. The interest inflow gives rise to a current account surplus and a trade deficit. Conversely, the low-saving country raises loans abroad. It pays interest on foreign debt. In order to finance the interest outflow, the country must be a net exporter of commodities. The interest outflow gives rise to a current account deficit and a trade surplus. The fast-growing country will be a debtor, the slow-growing country a creditor. If the foreign interest rate is high, the country will be a creditor. If the foreign interest rate is low, the country will be a debtor.

What are the dynamics of an increase in the saving rate? Initially the economy is in the steady state. The current account surplus per head and foreign assets per head are constant. Investment per head, capital per head and output per head do not move. The same applies to consumption per head and net imports per head. Against this background, the saving rate goes up. In the short run, the shock reduces consumption per head. It depresses net imports per head, thereby enhancing the current account surplus per head. Investment per head does not respond.

In the medium run, the rise in the current account surplus per head leads to the accumulation of foreign assets per head. Capital per head and output per head are invariant, since investment per head did not change. Owing to the expansion of foreign assets per head, the interest inflow per head swells. This augments the per-capita income of domestic residents and improves their consumption per head. The lift in consumption per head is accompanied by a lift in net imports per head. And the swell in the interest inflow per head brings up the current account surplus per head. In due course the economy reaches a new steady state. The current account surplus per head and foreign assets per head are again constant. As always investment per head, capital per head and output per head do not move. Consumption per head and net imports per head are once more uniform. Taking the sum over the process of adjustment as a whole, the current account surplus per head and foreign assets per head went up. Investment per head, capital per head and output per head did not react. Consumption per head and imports per head are larger than before.

We come next to a world consisting of two countries. What about the comparative statics? The high-saving country will be a creditor. It runs a current account surplus and a trade deficit. The other way round, the low-saving country will be a debtor. It runs a current account deficit and a trade surplus. Let country 1 be a creditor and country 2 a debtor. Now imagine an increase in the saving rate of country 1. In each of the countries, the shock raises capital per head and output per head. The foreign assets per head of country 1 pile up, as does the foreign debt per head of country 2. In both countries, as a rule, consumption per head becomes better, in the first line in country 1. This clearly differs from the conclusions drawn for the small open economy.

Symbols

A	assets
B	current account deficit
C	consumption
D	foreign debt
E	current account surplus
F	foreign assets
I	investment
K	capital
L	labour demand
N	labour supply
Q	net imports, trade deficit
S	savings
W	welfare
X	net exports, trade surplus
Y	output, income
Z	land

a	assets per head, parameter
b	current account deficit per head, parameter
c	consumption per head, parameter
d	foreign debt per head
e	current account surplus per head
f	foreign assets per head
g	function
h	function
i	investment per head
j	actual debt ratio
k	capital per head
m	maximum debt ratio
n	rate of labour growth
p	land rent
q	net imports per head

r	interest rate
s	saving rate
t	time
u	utility
v	capital-output ratio
w	wage rate
x	net exports per head
y	output per head, income per head
z	land per head

α	parameter of production function
β	parameter of production function
γ	parameter of utility function
δ	parameter of utility function
ε	efficiency
λ	speed of adjustment
ρ	discount rate
Π	profits

References

ALLAIS, M., Economie et Interet, Paris 1947

ALOGOSKOUFIS, G., VAN DER PLOEG, F., On Budgetary Policies, Growth and External Deficits in an Interdepentent World, in: Journal of the Japanese and International Economies 5, 1991, 305 - 324

AMANO, A., International Capital Movements and Economic Growth, in: Kyklos 18, 1965, 693 - 699

ANDERSON, T. M., MOENE, K. O., Eds., Endogenous Growth, 1993

ARMSTRONG, H. W., BALASUBRAMANYAM, V. N., SALISU, M. A., Domestic Savings, Intra-National and Intra-European Capital Flows, 1971 - 1991, in: European Economic Review 40, 1996, 1229 - 1235

AZARIADIS, C., Intertemporal Macroeconomics, Oxford 1993

BADE, R., Optimal Growth and Foreign Borrowing with Restricted Mobility of Foreign Capital, in: International Economic Review 13, 1972, 544 - 552

BARDHAN, P. K., Economic Growth, Development and Foreign Trade, New York 1974

BARDHAN, P. K., Equilibrium Growth in the International Economy, in: Quarterly Journal of Economics 79, 1965, 455 - 464

BARDHAN, P. K., Optimum Foreign Borrowing, in: K. Shell, Ed., Essays on the Theory of Optimal Economic Growth, Cambridge 1967

BARRO, R. J., Economic Growth in a Cross-Section of Countries, in: Quarterly Journal of Economics 106, 1991, 407 - 443

BARRO, R. J., MANKIW, N. G., SALA-I-MARTIN, X., Capital Mobility in Neoclassical Models of Growth, in: American Economic Review 85, 1995, 103 - 115

BARRO, R. J., SALA-I-MARTIN, X., Convergence, in: Journal Political Economy 100, 1992, 223 - 251

BARRO, R. J., SALA-I-MARTIN, X., Convergence Across States and Regions, in: Brookings Papers on Economic Activity 1, 1991, 107 - 158

BARRO, R. J., SALA-I-MARTIN, X., Economic Growth, New York 1995

BAUMOL, W. J., et al., Productivity and American Leadership: The Long View, Cambridge 1989

BAUMOL, W. J., Productivity Growth, Convergence and Welfare: What the Long-Run Data Show, in: American Economic Review 76, 1986, 1072 - 1085

BAZDARICH, M., Optimal Growth and Stages in the Balance of Payments, in: Journal of International Economics 8, 1978, 425 - 443

BERNARD, A. B., JONES, C. I., Technology and Convergence, in: Economic Journal 106, 1996, 1037 - 1044

BERNHEIM, B. D., SHOVEN, J. B., Eds., National Saving and Economic Performance, Chicago 1991

BERRY, R. A., SOLIGO, R., Some Welfare Aspects of International Migration, in: Journal of Political Economy 77, 1969, 778 - 794

BERTHOLD, N., Hg., Allgemeine Wirtschaftstheorie, München 1995

BERTHOLD, N., MODERY, W., Das Feldstein-Horioka-Paradoxon, in: Wirtschaftswissenschaftliches Studium 23, 1994, 492 - 497

BHAGWATI, J. N., Ed., Trade, Balance of Payments and Growth, Amsterdam 1971

BLANCHARD, O. J., FISCHER, S., Lectures on Macroeconomics, Cambridge 1989

BORJAS, G. J., The Economic Benefits from Immigration, in: Journal of Economic Perspectives 9, 1995, 3 - 22

BORTS, G., A Theory of Long-Run International Capital Movements, in: Journal of Political Economy 72, 1964, 341 - 359

BRAUN, J., Essays on Economic Growth and Migration, PhD Dissertation, Harvard University 1993

BRÄUNINGER, M., Generalised Social Security Finance in a Two-Country World, Discussion Paper, Hamburg 1995

BUITER, W. H., Time Preference and International Lending and Borrowing in an Overlapping Generations Model, in: Journal of Political Economy 89, 1981, 769 - 797

BUITER, W. H., KLETZER, K. M., Persistent Differences in National Productivity Growth Rates with a Common Technology and Free Capital Mobility: The Roles of Private Trift, Public Debt, Capital Taxation and Policy toward Human Capital Formation, in: Journal of the Japanese and International Economies 5, 1991, 325 - 353

BURDA, M., WYPLOSZ, C., Human Capital, Investment and Migration in an Integrated Europe, CEPR Discussion Paper 614, London 1991

BURDA, M., WYPLOSZ, C., Macroeconomics, Oxford 1993

BURMEISTER, E., DOBELL, R., Mathematical Theories of Economic Growth, New York 1970

CALVO, G. A., WELLISZ, S., International Factor Mobility and National Advantage, in: Journal of International Economics 14, 1983, 103 - 114

CARDOSO, E. A., DORNBUSCH, R., Foreign Private Capital Flows, in: H. B. Chenery, T. N. Srinivasan, Eds., Handbook of Development Economics, Amsterdam 1989

CARLBERG, M., Deutsche Vereinigung, Kapitalbildung und Beschäftigung, Heidelberg 1996

CARLBERG, M., Open Economy Dynamics, New York 1993

CARLBERG, M., Sustainability and Optimality of Public Debt, Heidelberg 1995

CHENERY, H. B., SRINIVASAN, T. N., Eds., Handbook of Development Economics, Amsterdam 1989

CHIANG, A. C., Elements of Dynamic Optimization, New York 1992

CHIANG, A. C., Fundamental Methods of Mathematical Economics, New York 1984

CLAASSEN, E. M., Monetäre Außenwirtschaftslehre, München 1996

COHEN, D., Growth and External Debt, in: F. van der Ploeg, Ed., Handbook of International Macroeconomics, Oxford 1994

COHEN, D., The Misfortunes of Prosperity, Cambridge 1996

COHEN, D., Private Lending to Sovereign States, Cambridge 1991

COHEN, D., SACHS, J. D., Growth and External Debt Under Risk of Debt Repudiation, in: European Economic Review 30, 1986, 529 - 560

COOPER, R. N., SACHS, J. D., Borrowing Abroad: The Debtor's Perspective, in: G. W. Smith, J. T. Cuddington, Eds., International Debt and the Developing Countries, Washington 1985

CRETTEZ, B., MICHEL, P., VIDAL, J. P., Time Preference and Factor Mobility in an OLG Model with Land, Discussion Paper, Liege 1996

DEI, F., Dynamic Gains from International Capital Movements, in: Journal of International Economics 9, 1979, 417 - 421

DEVEREUX, M., SHI, S., Capital Accumulation and the Current Account in a Two-Country Model, in: Journal of International Economics 30, 1991, 1 - 25

DIAMOND, P. A., National Debt in a Neoclassical Growth Model, in: American Economic Review 55, 1965, 1126 - 1150

DIECKHEUER, G., Internationale Wirtschaftsbeziehungen, München 1995

DIXIT, A. K., The Theory of Equilibrium Growth, Oxford 1982

DOMAR, E. D., The Effect of Foreign Investment on the Balance of Payments, in: American Economic Review 40, 1950, 805 - 826

DORNBUSCH, R., Dollars, Debts and Deficits, Cambridge 1986

202

DORNBUSCH, R., Intergenerational and International Trade, in: Journal of International Economics 18, 1985, 123 - 139

DORNBUSCH, R., FISCHER, S., The World Debt Problem: Origins and Prospects, in: Journal of Development Planning 16, 1985, 57 - 81

DOWRICK, S., NGUYEN, D., OECD Comparative Economic Growth 1950 - 1985: Catch-Up and Convergence, in: American Economic Review 79, 1989, 1010 - 1030

DURLAUF, S. N., On the Convergence and Divergence of Growth Rates: An Introduction, in: Economic Journal 106, 1996, 1016 - 1018

EATON, J., External Debt: A Primer, in: World Bank Economic Review 7, 1993, 137 - 172

EATON, J., Foreign Public Capital Flows, in: H. B. Chenery, T. N. Srinivasan, Eds., Handbook of Development Economics, Amsterdam 1989

EATON, J., FERNANDEZ, R., Sovereign Debt, in: G. M. Grossman, K. Rogoff, Eds., Handbook of International Economics, Amsterdam 1995

EATON, J., GERSOVITZ, M., STIGLITZ, J. E., The Pure Theory of Country Risk, in: European Economic Review 30, 1986, 481 - 513

EATON, J., PANAGARIYA, A., Growth and Welfare in a Small Open Economy, in: Economica 49, 1982, 409 - 419

EICHENGREEN, B., LINDERT, P. H., Eds., The International Debt Crisis in Historical Perspective, Cambridge 1989

FAGERBERG, J., Technology and International Differences in Growth Rates, in: Journal of Economic Literature 32, 1994, 1147 - 1175

FEDER, G., JUST, R. E., Optimal International Borrowing, Capital Allocation and Credit-Worthiness Control, in: Kredit und Kapital 12, 1979, 207 - 220

FEDER, G., REGEV, U., International Loans, Direct Foreign Investment, and Optimal Capital Accumulation, in: Economic Record 51, 1975, 320 - 325

FELDSTEIN, M., Domestic Saving and International Capital Movements in the Short Run and the Long Run, in: European Economic Review 21, 1983, 129 - 151

FELDSTEIN, M., Global Capital Flows, in: Economist, June 24th 1995, 90 - 91

FELDSTEIN, M., International Debt Service and Economic Growth - Some Simple Analytics, NBER Working Papers 2076, 1986

FELDSTEIN, M., Tax Policy and International Capital Flows, in: Weltwirtschaftliches Archiv 130, 1994, 675 - 697

FELDSTEIN, M., BACCHETTA, P., National Savings and International Investment, in: B. D. Bernheim, J. B. Shoven, Eds., National Saving and Economic Performance, Chicago 1991

FELDSTEIN, M., HORIOKA, C., Domestic Saving and International Capital Flows, in: Economic Journal 90, 1980, 314 - 329

FINN, M. G., On Savings and Investment Dynamics in a Small Open Economy, in: Journal of International Economics 29, 1990, 1 - 21

FISCHER, S., FRENKEL, J. A., Economic Growth and Stages of the Balance of Payments, in: G. Horwich, P. A. Samuelson, Eds., Trade, Stability and Macroeconomics, New York 1974

FISCHER, S., FRENKEL, J. A., Interest Rate Equalization and Patterns of Production, Trade and Consumption in a Two-Country Growth Model, in: Economic Record 50, 1974, 555 - 580

FISCHER, S., FRENKEL, J. A., Investment, the Two-Sector Model and Trade in Debt and Capital Goods, in: Journal of International Economics 2, 1972, 211 - 233

FRENKEL, J. A., Ed., Internationalization of Equity Markets, Chicago 1994

FRENKEL, J. A., DOOLEY, M. P., WICKHAM, P., Eds., Analytical Issues in Debt, Washington 1989

FRENKEL, J. A., FISCHER, S., International Capital Movements along Balanced Growth Paths: Comments and Extensions, in: Economic Record 48, 1972, 266 - 271

FRENKEL, J. A., RAZIN, A., Fiscal Policies and the World Economy, Cambridge 1992

FRIED, J., The Intergenerational Distribution of the Gains from Technological Change and from International Trade, in: Canadian Journal of Economics 13, 1980, 65 - 81

FRIEDMAN, M., Do Old Fallacies Ever Die?, in: Journal of Economic Literature 30, 1992, 2129 - 2132

GAHLEN, B., HESSE, H., RAMSER, H. J., Hg., Europäische Integrationsprobleme aus wirtschaftswissenschaftlicher Sicht, Tübingen 1994

GAHLEN, B., HESSE, H., RAMSER, H. J., Hg., Wachstumstheorie und Wachstumspolitik, Tübingen 1991

GALE, D., General Equilibrium with Imbalance of Trade, in: Journal of International Economics 1, 1971, 141 - 158

GALE, D., The Trade Imbalance Story, in: Journal of International Economics 4, 1974, 119 - 137

GALOR, O., The Choice of Factor Mobility in a Dynamic World, in: Journal of Population Economics 5, 1992, 135 - 144

GALOR, O., Convergence: Inferences from Theoretical Models, in: Economic Journal 106, 1996, 1056 - 1069

GANDOLFO, G., Economic Dynamics, Berlin 1996

GANDOLFO, G., International Economics, Berlin 1995

GHOSH, A. R., International Capital Mobility Amongst the Major Industrialised Countries, in: Economic Journal 105, 1995, 107 - 128

GIAVAZZI, F., WYPLOSZ, C., The Zero Root Problem: A Note on the Dynamic Determination of the Stationary Equilibrium in Linear Models, in: Review of Economic Studies 52, 1985, 352 - 357

GREEN, J., The Question of Collective Rationality in Professor Gale's Model of Trade Imbalance, in: Journal of International Economics 2, 1972, 39 - 55

GRINOLS, E., BHAGWATI, J. N., Foreign Capital, Savings and Dependence, in: Review of Economics and Statistics 58, 1976, 416 - 424

GRINOLS, E., BHAGWATI, J. N., Foreign Capital, Savings and Dependence: A Reply to Mr. Wasow, in: Review of Economics and Statistics 61, 1979, 154 - 156

GROSSMAN, G. M., The Gains from International Factor Movements, in: Journal of International Economics 17, 1984, 73 - 83

GROSSMAN, G. M., HELPMAN, E., Endogenous Innovation in the Theory of Growth, in: Journal of Economic Perspectives 8, 1994, 23 - 44

GROSSMAN, G. M., HELPMAN, E., Innovation and Growth in the Global Economy, Cambridge 1991

GROSSMAN, G. M., ROGOFF, K., Eds., Handbook of International Economics, Amsterdam 1995

GROßMANN, H., Auslandsverschuldung, Terms of Trade und überlappende Generationen, Frankfurt 1990

HAHN, F., SOLOW, R., A Critical Essay on Modern Macroeconomic Theory, Oxford 1995

HAMADA, K., Economic Growth and Long-Term International Capital Movements, in: Yale Economic Essays 6, 1966, 49 - 96

HAMADA, K., Optimal Capital Accumulation by an Economy Facing an International Capital Market, in: Journal of Political Economy 77, 1969, 684 - 697

HANSON, J. A., Optimal International Borrowing and Lending, in: American Economic Review 64, 1974, 616 - 630

HANSON, J. A., NEHER, P. A., The Neoclassical Theorem Once Again: Closed and Open Economies, in: American Economic Review 57, 1967, 869 - 878

HAX, H., Ed., Economic Transformation in Eastern Europe and East Asia - A Challenge for Japan and Germany, Berlin 1995

HOMBURG, S., Efficient Economic Growth, Berlin 1992

HORI, H., STEIN, J. L., International Growth with Free Trade in Equities and Goods, in: International Economic Review 19, 1977, 83 - 100

HORWICH, G., SAMUELSON, P. A., Eds., Trade, Stability and Macroeconomics, New York 1974

IHORI, T., Public Finance in an Overlapping Generations Economy, London 1996

ISSING, O., MASUCH, K., Zur Frage der normativen Interpretation von Leistungsbilanzsalden, in: Kredit und Kapital 22, 1989, 1 - 17

JONES, L., MANUELLI, R., A Convex Model of Equilibrium Growth, in: Journal of Political Economy 98, 1990, 1008 - 1038

JONES, R. W., KENEN, P. B., Eds., Handbook of International Economics, Amsterdam 1985

KAREKEN, J., WALLACE, N., Portfolio Autarky: A Welfare Analysis, in: Journal of International Economics 7, 1977, 19 - 43

KEMP, M. C., Foreign Investment and the National Advantage, in: Economic Record 38, 1962, 56 - 62

KEMP, M. C., International Trade and Investment in a Context of Growth, in: Economic Record 44, 1968, 211 - 223

KEMP, M. C., International Trade Between Countries with Different Natural Rates of Growth, in: Economic Record 46, 1970, 467 - 481

KENEN, P. B., Economic and Monetary Union, Cambridge 1995

KENEN, P. B., Ed., Understanding Interdependence, Princeton 1995

KHANG, C., Equilibrium Growth in the International Economy: The Case of Unequal Natural Rates of Growth, in: International Economic Review 12, 1971, 239 - 249

KING, R. J., REBELO, S. T., Transitional Dynamics and Economic Growth in the Neoclassical Model, in: American Economic Review 83, 1993, 908 - 931

KLETZER, K. M., Sovereign Immunity and International Lending, in: F. van der Ploeg, Ed., Handbook of International Macroeconomics, Oxford 1994

KOIZUMI, T., KOPECKY, K. J., Economic Growth, Capital Movements and the International Transfer of Technical Knowledge, in: Journal of International Economics 7, 1977, 45 - 65

KRELLE, W., The Future of the World Economy, Berlin 1989

KRELLE, W., Theorie des wirtschaftlichen Wachstum, Berlin 1988

KRUEGER, T. H., OSTRY, J. D., Exercises in Intertemporal Open-Economy Macroeconomics, Cambridge 1993

KRUGMAN, P., Pop Internationalism, Cambridge 1996

KRUGMAN, P. R., OBSTFELD, M., International Economics, New York 1994

KURZ, M., The General Instability of a Class of Competitive Growth Processes, in: Review of Economic Studies 35, 1968, 155 - 174

LAITNER, J., Transition Time Paths for Overlapping Generations Models, in: Journal of Economic Dynamics and Control 7, 1984, 111 - 129

LEE, C. J., Capital Movements, Growth and the Balance of Payments, in: Journal of Macroeconomics 4, 1982, 433 - 447

LEIDERMAN, L., RAZIN, A., Eds., Capital Mobility - The Impact on Consumption, Investment and Growth, Cambridge 1994

LESLIE, D., Advanced Macroeconomics, New York 1993

LEWIS, K. K., Puzzles in International Financial Markets, in: G. M. Grossman, K. Rogoff, Eds., Handbook of International Economics, Amsterdam 1995

LUCAS, R. E., On the Mechanics of Economic Development, in: Journal of Monetary Economics 22, 1988, 3 - 42

LUCAS, R., Why Doesn't Capital Flow from Rich to Poor Countries?, in: American Economic Review, Papers and Proceedings 80, 1990, 92 - 96

MACDOUGALL, G. D. A., The Benefits and Costs of Private Investment Abroad, in: Economic Record 36, 1960, 13 - 35

MADDISON, A., Monitoring the World Economy 1820 - 1992, Washington 1995

MANKIW, N. G., ROMER, D., WEIL, D. N., A Contribution to the Empirics of Economic Growth, in: Quarterly Journal of Economics 107, 1992, 407 - 437

MATSUYAMA, K., Current Account Dynamics in a Finite Horizon Model, in: Journal of International Economics 23, 1987, 299 - 313

MCCALLUM, B. T., International Monetary Economics, Oxford 1995

MOHR, E., Economic Theory and Sovereign International Debt, New York 1991

MÜLLER, H. W., Staatliche Auslandsverschuldung und internationale Kapitalbewegungen, Frankfurt 1992

MUNDELL, R. A., International Economics, New York 1968

MURPHY, R. G., Capital Mobility and the Relationship between Saving and Investment in OECD countries, in: Journal of International Money and Finance 3, 1984, 327 - 342

MYERS, M. G., Equilibrium Growth and Capital Movements between Open Economies, in: American Economic Review, Papers and Proceedings 60, 1970, 393 - 397

MYERS, M. G., Equilibrium Growth and Capital Movements in Open Economies, PhD Dissertation, Brown University 1969

NEGISHI, T., Foreign Investment and the Long-Run National Advantage, in: Economic Record 41, 1965, 628 - 632

NEHER, P. A., Economic Growth and Development, New York 1971

NEHER, P. A., International Capital Movements along Balanced Growth Paths, in: Economic Record 46, 1970, 393 - 401

NEUMANN, M., Theoretische Volkswirtschaftslehre, München 1995

NEUMANN, M., Zukunftsperspektiven im Wandel, Tübingen 1990

NIEHANS, J., Geschichte der Außenwirtschaftstheorie im Überblick, Tübingen 1995

NIKAIDO, H., Prices, Cycles, and Growth, Cambridge 1996

OBSTFELD, M., Capital Mobility in the World Economy: Theory and Measurement, in: Carnegie-Rochester Conference Series 24, 1986, 55 - 104

OBSTFELD, M., International Capital Mobility in the 1990s, in: P. B. Kenen, Ed., Understanding Interdependence, Princeton 1995

OBSTFELD, M., ROGOFF, K., Foundations of International Macroeconomics, Cambridge 1996

OBSTFELD, M., ROGOFF, K., The Intertemporal Approach to the Current Account, in: G. M. Grossmann, K. Rogoff, Eds., Handbook of International Economics, Amsterdam 1995

ONITSUKA, Y., International Capital Movements and the Patterns of Economic Growth, in: American Economic Review 64, 1974, 24 - 36

PACK, H., Endogenous Growth Theory: Intellectual Appeal and Empirical Shortcomings, in: Journal of Economic Perspectives 8, 1994, 55 - 72

PERSSON, T., Deficits and Intergenerational Welfare in Open Economies, in: Journal of International Economics 19, 1985, 67 - 84

VAN DER PLOEG, F., Ed., Handbook of International Macroeconomics, Oxford 1994

VAN DER PLOEG, F., TANG, P., Growth, Deficits, and Research and Development in the Global Economy, in: F. van der Ploeg, Ed., Handbook of International Macroeconomics, Oxford 1994

VAN DER PLOEG, F., TANG, P. J. G., The Macroeconomics of Growth: An International Perspective, in: Oxford Review of Economic Policy 8, 1992, 15 - 28

QUAH, D., Convergence Empirics with (Some) Capital Mobility, in: Journal of Economic Growth 1996, Forthcoming

QUAH, D., Empirics for Economic Growth and Convergence, in: European Economic Review 40, 1996, 1353 - 1375

QUAH, D. T., Twin-Peaks: Growth and Convergence in Models of Distribution Dynamics, in: Economic Journal 106, 1996, 1045 - 1055

RAMSER, H. J., Wachstumstheorie, in: N. Berthold, Hg., Allgemeine Wirtschaftstheorie, München 1995

RAMSEY, F. P., A Mathematical Theory of Saving, in: Economic Journal 38, 1928, 543 - 559

REBELO, S., Growth in Open Economies, in: Carnegie-Rochester Conference Series on Public Policy 36, 1992, 5 - 46

REBELO, S., Long-Run Policy Analysis and Long-Run Growth, in: Journal of Political Economy 99, 1991, 500 - 521

RIEß, A. D., Optimale Auslandsverschuldung bei potentiellen Schuldendienstproblemen, Frankfurt 1988

RIVERA-BATIZ, L. A., ROMER, P. M., Economic Integration and Endogenous Growth, in: Quarterly Journal of Economics 106, 1991, 531 - 555

ROMER, D., Advanced Macroeconomics, New York 1996

ROMER, P. M., Capital Accumulation in the Theory of Long-Run Growth, in: R. J. Barro, Ed., Modern Business Cycle Theory, Oxford 1989

ROMER, P. M., Increasing Returns and Long-Run Growth, in: Journal of Political Economy 94, 1986, 1002 - 1037

ROMER, P. M., The Origins of Endogenous Growth, in: Journal of Economic Perspectives 8, 1994, 3 - 22

RUFFIN, R. J., Growth and the Long-Run Theory of International Capital Movements, in: American Economic Review 69, 1979, 832 - 842

RUSCHINSKI, M., Neuere Entwicklungen in der Wachstumstheorie, Wiesbaden 1996

SACHS, J. D., Theoretical Issues in International Borrowing, Princeton Studies in International Finance 54, Princeton 1984

SALA-I-MARTIN, X., The Classical Approach to Convergence Analysis, in: Economic Journal 106, 1996, 1019 - 1036

SALA-I-MARTIN, X., On the Growth and States, PhD Dissertation, Harvard University 1990

SALA-I-MARTIN, X., Regional Cohesion: Evidence and Theories of Regional Growth and Convergence, in: European Economic Review 40, 1996, 1325 - 1352

SCHLICHT, E., Die Wachstumstheorie im Widerspiel von Mikro- und Makroansatz, in: Gahlen, B., u. a., Hg., Wachstumstheorie und Wachstumspolitik, Tübingen 1991

SCHMID, M., GROßMANN, H., Auslandsverschuldung im Modell mit überlappenden Generationen, in: R. Ertel, H. J. Heinemann, Hg., Aspekte internationaler Wirtschaftsbeziehungen, Hannover 1986

SCHMITT-RINK, G., BENDER, D., Makroökonomie geschlossener und offener Volkswirtschaften, Berlin 1992

SCHNEIDER, H., Optimales Wachstum und Auslandsverschuldung, Arbeitspapier, Zürich 1984

SCHNEIDER, J., ZIESEMER, T., What's New and What's Old in New Growth Theory, in: Zeitschrift für Wirtschafts- und Sozialwissenschaften 115, 1995, 429 - 472

SCOTT, M. F., A New View of Economic Growth, Oxford 1989

SEN, P., Savings, Investment, and the Current Account, in: F. van der Ploeg, Ed., Handbook of International Macroeconomics, Oxford 1994

SIEBERT, H., Foreign Debt and Capital Accumulation, in: Weltwirtschaftliches Archiv 123, 1987, 618 - 630

SIEBERT, H., The Half and the Full Debt Cycle, in: Weltwirtschaftliches Archiv 125, 1989, 217 - 229

SIEBERT, H., Ed., Locational Competition in the World Economy, Tübingen 1995

SIMON, J. L., The Economic Consequences of Immigration, Oxford 1989

SMITH, G. D., CUDDINGTON, J. T., Eds., International Debt and the Developing Countries, Washington 1985

SOLOW, R. M., A Contribution to the Theory of Economic Growth, in: Quarterly Journal of Economics 70, 1956, 65 - 94

SOLOW, R. M., New Directions in Growth Theory, in: Gahlen, B., u.a., Hg., Wachstumstheorie und Wachstumspolitik, Tübingen 1991

SOLOW, R. M., Perspectives on Growth Theory, in: Journal of Economic Perspectives 8, 1994, 45 - 54

STEINMANN, G., The Effects of Immigrants on the Income of Natives, in: G. Steinmann, R. E. Ulrich, Eds., The Economic Consequences of Immigration to Germany, Heidelberg 1994

STEINMANN, G., ULRICH, R. E., Eds., The Economic Consequences of Immigration to Germany, Heidelberg 1994

STIGLITZ, J. E., Factor Price Equalization in a Dynamic Economy, in: Journal of Political Economy 78, 1970, 456 - 488

TESAR, L. L., WERNER, I. M., Home Bias and the Globalization of Securities Markets, in: J. Frenkel, Ed., Internationalization of Equity Markets, Chicago 1994

TURNOVSKY, S. J., Ed., Intertemporal Issues in International Macroeconomics, Amsterdam 1991

TURNOVSKY, S. J., Methods of Macroeconomic Dynamics, Cambridge 1995

UTECHT, B., Neoklassische Wachstumstheorie, Freihandel und internationaler Kapitalverkehr, Berlin 1996

VAN LONG, N., SIEBERT, H., Optimal Foreign Borrowing: Sensitivity Analysis with Respect to the Planning Horizon, in: Journal of Economics 49, 1989, 279 - 297

VIDAL, J. P., Capital Mobility in a Dynamic Framework, Discussion Paper, Paris 1996

VOSGERAU, H. J., Die Internationalisierung der Wirtschaft in ihrer Bedeutung für das Wirtschaftswachstum, in: Gahlen, B., u. a., Hg., Wachstumstheorie und Wachstumspolitik, Tübingen 1991

WAGNER, H., Europäische Wirtschaftspolitik, Berlin 1995

WAGNER, H., Wachstum und Entwicklung, München 1993

WALZ, U., Growth Effects of Migration, in: Zeitschrift für Wirtschafts- und Sozialwissenschaften 115, 1995, 199 - 221

WAN, H. Y., Economic Growth, New York 1971

WAN, H. Y., A Simultaneous Variational Model for International Capital Movements, in: J. N. Bhagwati, Ed., Trade, Balance of Payments and Growth, Amsterdam 1971

WASOW, B., Savings and Dependence with Externally Financed Growth, in: Review of Economics and Statistics 61, 1979, 150 - 154

WEIL, P., Essays on the Valuation of Unbacked Assets, PhD Thesis, Harvard University 1985

INDEX